The Rapid Deployment Force
and U.S. Military Intervention
in the Persian Gulf

Jeffrey Record

Special Report

May 1983, Second Edition

INSTITUTE FOR FOREIGN POLICY ANALYSIS, INC.
Cambridge, Massachusetts, and Washington, D.C.

Requests for copies of IFPA Special Reports should be addressed to the Circulation Manager, Special Reports, Institute for Foreign Policy Analysis, Central Plaza Building, Tenth Floor, 675 Massachusetts Avenue, Cambridge, Massachusetts 02139 (Telephone: 617-492-2116). Please send a check or money order for the correct amount along with your order.

Standing orders for all Special Reports will be accepted by the Circulation Manager. Standing order subscribers will automatically receive all future Special Reports as soon as they are published. Each Report will be accompanied by an invoice.

IFPA also maintains a **mailing list** of individuals and institutions who are notified periodically of new Institute publications. Those desiring to be placed on this list should write to the Circulation Manager, Special Reports, at the above address.

A list of IFPA publications appears on the inside back cover.

Printed by Corporate Press, Inc., Washington, D.C.

Contents

Preface

In November 1980, the Institute for Foreign Policy Analysis published *Force Reductions in Europe: Starting Over,* a Special Report by Dr. Jeffrey Record, Senior Fellow of the Institute for Foreign Policy Analysis in its Washington office. The present study is the second of several such Special Reports that will be prepared by Dr. Record; and it is also one of a series of monographs to be published by the Institute which will examine the defense problems associated with Western dependence on the oil and non-fuel minerals of Africa and the Persian Gulf. Future studies by Dr. Record will examine other important security issues, including theater nuclear modernization in Europe, confronting the United States in the 1980s. Like other Special Reports of the Institute, these studies by Dr. Record are designed to contribute to a broader understanding of the international security environment and principal policy issues and options for the United States in the years just ahead.

This is to acknowledge with gratitude support to the Institute for Foreign Policy Analysis for Dr. Record's research, which has been provided by the Earhart Foundation and the Samuel Roberts Noble Foundation.

Robert L. Pfaltzgraff, Jr.
President
Institute for Foreign Policy Analysis

Summary Overview

The Rapid Deployment Force (RDF) formed by the Carter Administration in the wake of the Soviet invasion of Afghanistan in December 1979 is a fatally flawed military instrument for the preservation of uninterrupted U.S. access to vital Persian Gulf oil—the principal rationale underlying the force. Indeed, the RDF is not a force as such, but rather a hastily-thrown together collection of existing units based in the United States. Most of these units are already earmarked for contingencies outside the Gulf region and improperly equipped or structured for the exacting demands of desert warfare against large and often mechanized potential adversaries in a logistically remote area of the world.

The RDF suffers from inadequate strategic and tactical mobility as well as forcible-entry capability. It is further plagued by a confused and divided command apparatus stemming from an unusually vicious interservice rivalry (primarily between the U.S. Army and the Marine Corps) for control of the rapid deployment mission.

The central condition confronting any U.S. attempt to mount a credible military defense of its economic interests in the Gulf region is the lack of assured military access ashore. Unlike our allies in Europe and Northwest Asia, friendly regimes in the Gulf region are unwilling to permit the establishment in peacetime of an operationally significant U.S. military presence on their territory, for fear that such a presence would compromise their internal political legitimacy. This fear is fully justified, and a governing principle of any U.S. military intervention in the Gulf should be the avoidance at all costs of the kind of Vietnam-style, massive logistical presence on land that invariably excites the hostility of indigenous nationalism. Unfortunately, the RDF is composed largely of U.S. Army and Air Force units whose commitment to combat in the Persian Gulf would be critically dependent on pre-hostilities access to bases and airfields ashore and would require the creation ashore of a huge support infrastructure. In effect, the RDF's success or failure in wartime has been staked on the momentary political calculations of potential host regimes in the Gulf.

The deficiencies of the Rapid Deployment Force can be overcome only through the replacement of the present force by a small, agile, tactically capable intervention force that is based at and supplied from the sea; controlled by a single, unified command; and supported by expanded sea power, especially forcible-entry capabilities. Such an intervention force would stress quality at the expense of size; immediate responsiveness at the expense of delayed augmentation from the United States;

sea-based power projection capabilities at the expense of air-transported Army forces and land-based tactical air power; and logistical self-sufficiency at the expense of dependence on facilities ashore.

Such a force can be created by

- transferring responsibility for the rapid deployment mission to the U.S. Marine Corps, which by virtue of its traditions and capabilities is the only service suitable for the mission;

- establishing, in the form of a new, 5th Fleet, a unified U.S. command with jurisdiction over the whole Indian Ocean and Persian Gulf region;

- increasing reliance on the concept of maritime prepositioning beyond that now planned;

- acquiring lightweight armored fighting vehicles and adopting a maneuver warfare operational doctrine;

- developing sea-based logistical systems capable of supplying and maintaining RDF units committed ashore; and

- increasing present levels of amphibious shipping and naval gunfire support capabilities.

Realization of these measures will entail substantial expenditures. Moreover, the U.S. Navy's inability to recruit and retain sufficient numbers of qualified personnel to man the existing fleet suggests that the expansion in U.S. sea power necessary to provide a credible Rapid Deployment Force cannot be achieved within the framework of the All-Volunteer Force.

If, however, the United States is serious about mounting a convincing military defense of threatened interests in the Persian Gulf, it cannot escape hard budgetary and social choices. The decision to commit the United States to a defense of those interests already has been made. What is lacking is the ability to do so.

1. Introduction

Any attempt by any outside force to gain control of the Persian Gulf region will be regarded as an assault on the vital interests of the United States of America, and such an assault will be repelled by any means necessary, including military force.

So declared President Carter in his January 20, 1980 State of the Union message, in what quickly became labeled the "Carter Doctrine." During the following months the Administration sought to provide the doctrine a credible military foundation through a series of budgetary, organizational, and foreign policy initiatives aimed not at expanding or restructuring U.S. forces but rather at increasing the speed with which existing U.S. military units could be deployed to the logistically remote Gulf region and the ability to provision those units upon their arrival. The initiatives included budget requests for specialized logistics ships and a new strategic transport aircraft; the establishment of a new headquarters—the Rapid Deployment Joint Task Force—charged with identifying, training, and planning the employment of units suitable for rapid deployment; and the launching of negotiations with several countries in the Gulf region for contingent access to military facilities.

That the uninterrupted flow of oil from the Persian Gulf constitutes a threatened and inadequately defended vital U.S. interest in the region is not in dispute. As then Secretary of Defense Harold Brown testified in 1980 before the House Foreign Affairs Committee,

what is at stake in the Persian Gulf is economic and political well-being of the United States and its allies. If the industrialized nations of the world were deprived of access to the energy resources of the Gulf, the results . . . would very probably be collapse of our allies and the world economy.[1]

This study addresses the question of whether that cluster of programs and initiatives known as the Rapid Deployment Force provides a credible military defense of "access to the energy resources of the . . . Gulf." It is the central thesis of this study that

(1) *the Rapid Deployment Force currently envisaged by the Department of Defense is a fatally flawed instrument for effective U.S. military intervention in the Persian Gulf;*

---

[1]*Aerospace Daily*, February 20, 1980, p. 265.

1

(2) *its flaws are attributable in part to the inherent political obstacles to successful intervention in the Gulf, and in part to the structural, technological, and doctrinal unsuitability of rapidly deployable U.S. forces for the likely combat environments they would confront in the region; and*

(3) *fundamental alterations both in the concept of military intervention and in the character of the Rapid Deployment Force itself are required if the strategic commitment enunciated in the Carter Doctrine is to be convincingly supported by military power.*

In the author's judgment, the present Rapid Deployment Force (RDF) is a standing invitation to military disaster—a disaster from which the military reputation of the United States, already battered by thirty years of defeats and miscarriages, would have difficulty recovering. As currently constituted, the RDF is little more than a *hodgepodge of improperly equipped and structured units lumped together under a confused command apparatus rent by unusually vicious and debilitating interservice rivalry for domination of the rapid deployment mission.*

Worse still is the potential scope of military intervention implied by the composition of the RDF: a force of up to 200,000 active troops augmented by the call-up of no fewer than 100,000 reservists. Even to contemplate committing such a force to land combat in the Persian Gulf region ignores one of the principal lessons of Vietnam—namely, that the very creation of a massive American military presence ashore in the Third World is likely to be self-defeating because it excites powerful local nationalism invariably hostile to that presence.

Indeed, avoidance of a massive armed presence ashore should be a governing principle of U.S. strategy in the greater Middle East, a region long consumed by virulent and profoundly anti-Western nationalism. The adverse operational consequences of that nationalism for the RDF are already manifest in the refusal of even such friendly states as Egypt and Oman to permit the peacetime stationing on their own territory of any U.S. combat contingents. To do so would invite internal challenges of the kind that toppled the Shah of Iran.

The United States must therefore avoid a traditional form of American military intervention in the non-Western world, an intervention characterized by the application of massive military power directly against a local state on its own territory or on behalf of a regime incapable of maintaining itself without the presence of foreign bayonets.

The primary aim of U.S. military intervention in the Gulf should be to prevent the region from becoming forcibly dominated by a single power, be that power the Soviet Union, Iraq, or some other Gulf state. More importantly, intervention must be conducted in a fashion that does not give rise to perceptions that the United States itself seeks hegemony. In short, the United States must, to paraphrase a Chinese axiom, oppose domination without seeking to dominate or appearing to dominate.

Accordingly, what is needed as an instrument of intervention is a force capable of defending the oil-producing states from attacks by each other or by Soviet or Soviet-sponsored forces, while simultaneously maintaining a low political profile in the host country. To be more specific, what is *not* needed is a large, unwieldy combat force that, in the classic American expeditionary tradition, is able to sustain itself only through the presence ashore of an even larger logistical support infrastructure. What *is* needed is a small, agile force, based at and supplied entirely from the sea. The model must be Sir John Moore's (and later Wellington's) sea-based strike force hovering off the Iberian peninsula, not Westmoreland's sprawling military bureaucracy in Vietnam.

Strategic mobility—getting U.S. forces to the Gulf in time—is not enough. Upon arrival, those forces must be capable of defeating larger, often mechanized, and heavily-armored opponents, and doing so unencumbered politically or militarily by the presence ashore of a long logistical tail. These twin capabilities can be gained only by providing the RDF what it now lacks: organizational, battlefield and logistical *agility.* In the author's view, this agility can be achieved only through (1) the permanent assignment of responsibility for the rapid deployment mission to a single service—the Marine Corps, which by virtue of its traditions, capabilities, and intellectual outlook is the only service suitable for the mission; (2) an increase in tactical mobility through the acquisition of new lightweight armored fighting vehicles and adoption of an operational doctrine of maneuver warfare; and (3) the development of sea-based logistical capabilities able to supply and maintain ground forces ashore. These measures, together with selected increases in amphibious assault capability and greater-than-planned investment in maritime prepositioning, would provide the United States a truly effective instrument of military power in the Persian Gulf. The hallmark of a proper RDF would be its reliance on the likely U.S. advantage in sea power.

At stake is not just the character of a specific military force but the efficacy of America's traditional style of warfare, a style predicated on the possession of resource superiority on the battlefield and aimed at the sheer physical destruction of enemy forces through the delivery of overwhelming firepower against them. Unfortunately, the so-called "firepower/attrition" approach to warfare entails a very low ratio of combat to support formations; heavy reliance on firepower requires an enormous supply train to feed the "firepower machines," and, in fact, the United States Army has the lowest "tooth-to-tail" ratio of any major ground force in the world. An equally significant weakness of firepower/attrition is its inherent disutility against an adversary possessing greater firepower. As in a boxing ring, the smaller contender cannot rely on brute strength to beat the larger, more muscle-bound opponent; to win, he must be more agile and use what strength he has in a more intelligent and effective manner. In essence, he must *outmaneuver* him.

In any Persian Gulf contingency involving either Soviet forces or the Soviet-model armies of Iraq or Syria, U.S. forces could expect to be substantially outnumbered and outgunned, as have been NATO forces for years in Central Europe. Thus, a prerequisite for any effective RDF must be the abandonment of firepower/attrition; it is a recipe for defeat in the face of potential adversaries possessing a pronounced superiority in virtually all of the measurable indices of military power, which regrettably are still widely regarded in the Pentagon as the indices most worthy of consideration.

What must be adopted in place of firepower/attrition is a style of warfare that would truly enable the United States to "fight outnumbered and win"—the maneuver style of warfare, which, as both the Germans and Israelis have repeatedly demonstrated since 1940, permits a smaller force to defeat a larger one and often without significant risk of protracted conflict associated with firepower/attrition. The aim of maneuver warfare is not the destruction of enemy forces as such, but the disruption of the enemy's internal cohesion and expectations of combat—i.e., his capacity to *use* his forces *effectively*—by using surprise, stealth, and rapid move-ment to present him with a succession of unexpected and dangerous situations more rapidly than he can react to them. It is perhaps more than coincidental that the Marine Corps, the smallest and most austere of the services, has shown greater interest in the concept of maneuver warfare than any other service, and is now actively experimenting with new tac-tical doctrines and equipment based upon the concept.

The following chapter analyzes the types of violent threats to assured Western access to Persian Gulf oil that might prompt U.S. military inter-vention. Chapter 3 explores the formidable political and military obsta-cles to—and concommitant requirements for—successful U.S. military intervention in the Gulf. The present Rapid Deployment Force is reviewed in Chapter 4, followed by an assessment of its deficiencies in Chapter 5. The final chapter proposes an alternative instrument of intervention.

The focus of this study on the requirements for effective U.S. military intervention in the Persian Gulf should be interpreted by the reader neither as a predilection for primary reliance on military options as a means of fostering the uninterrupted production and flow of oil from the Gulf, nor as a conviction that the United States alone can, or should, bear the burden of defending this vital Western interest.

In an area as fragmented, unstable, politicized, and wary of, as well as vulnerable to, external intrusions as is the Middle East, a defense policy that relies in the main on a military instrumentality to create collective security is bound to prove inadequate, unless the political foundations, on which any multinational effort must rest, are solid. The record of American Middle East policy since World War II strongly suggests that the *real* regional security challenge for the United States lies in a proper orchestration of military implements on the one hand, and political relationships with our regional partners on the other. This is a most difficult task. But it is indispensable if the regional use of U.S. military power . . . is not to be frustrated in the moment of need by the unwillingness or inability of local governments to do their share.[2]

Oil fields are by their nature difficult to defend, and means less costly than military force are available to the United States for reducing economic sensitivity at least to temporary interruptions in supply. Determined and comprehensive efforts to eliminate wasteful consumption (requiring perhaps a stiff tariff on imported oil), to develop other sources of energy, and to establish a truly meaningful strategic petroleum stockpile are essential to any effective U.S. "grand strategy" in the Gulf, and could obviate the need for precipitate military action in the event of disruption. These measures, if supplemented by a U.S. Middle East diplomacy more cognizant of the influence of the U.S.-Israeli relationship upon Arab perceptions of American purpose in the region, and by carefully calibrated security and technical assistance programs designed to bolster the political stability and self-defense capabilities of selected oil-producing states, would serve to enhance deterrence of those who would challenge Western interests in the Gulf by force. They cannot, however, guarantee deterrence against aggression, and it is the prospect of failed deterrence that demands a willingness to use force and the ability to use it effectively.

Western programs to curb oil consumption and to develop alternate sources of energy, even if pursued with uncharacteristic vigor, are not likely in our lifetime to eliminate the dependence of the industrial world, particularly Europe and Japan, on Persian Gulf oil. Moreover, the Soviet

---

[2]Paul Jabber, "U.S. Interests and Regional Security in the Middle East," *Daedalus,* Fall 1980, pp. 68-69.

Union itself, long a net exporter of oil and natural gas, is expected to become a major competitor for Gulf oil well before the end of the century.

The issue of who should bear the burden of defending the Gulf is conditioned by two inescapable realities. The first is that the United States is militarily in no position to do so alone without significantly degrading its longstanding commitments to the defense of Europe and the Far East. The second is that Western Europe and Japan, which are far more dependent on Gulf oil than the United States (as illustrated in Table 1), are capable of making substantial, if largely indirect, contributions to the region's defense. Those potential contributions include greater self-defense efforts, thereby "releasing" U.S. forces for the Gulf; participation in a joint standing naval force in the Indian Ocean; provision of airfield and port facilities (both in Europe and in the Middle East) to support operations in the Gulf; dedication of support ships and maritime patrol aircraft to supplement limited U.S. supply and surveillance capabilities in the Indian Ocean; and provision of financial support to RDF-related military construction projects in the Middle East.[3]

Needless to say, both Europe and Japan are capable of providing substantial development aid and technical assistance to internally beleaguered regimes in the greater Gulf region. Given the nature of the most immediate threats to assured Western access to Persian Gulf oil, non-military responses to the crisis in the Gulf may prove far more effective in the long run than the kind of military response embodied in the Rapid Deployment Force.

---

[3]For an exploration of these and other political Allied contributions to the defense of the Gulf, see Dov Zakheim, "Of Allies and Access," *The Washington Quarterly*, Winter 1981.

TABLE 1

The Economic Importance of Oil Imported from the Persian Gulf: Selected OECD States' Petroleum Product Imports as a Percentage of Petroleum Product Consumption Plus Exports, 1979

(In thousands of metric tons, ranking by percentage)

Country	Imports (I) from Persian Gulf[1]			Consumption (C)	Exports (E)	C+E	I/C+E
	Crude/NGL/Feedstocks	Total Products	Total				
France	92,962	1,322	94,284	103,016	16,039	119,055	.792
Japan	156,429	9,891	166,320	243,478	353	243,831	.682
Italy	72,774	1,433	74,207	89,316	22,530	111,846	.663
Netherlands	39,871	1,294	41,165	28,993	43,979	72,972	.564
New Zealand	1,709	15	1,724	3,365	40	3,405	.506
United Kingdom	47,104	231	47,335	81,490	12,993	94,483	.501
Belgium	19,761	86	19,847	24,738	15,252	39,990	.496
Australia	8,329	1,161	9,490	27,479	1,758	29,237	.325
Federal Republic of Germany	42,491	568	43,059	132,202	6,675	138,877	.310
United States	114,693	769	115,462	731,598	13,529	745,127	.155
Canada	13,388	—	13,388	82,076	5,743	87,619	.152

Source: OECD, Quarterly Oil Statistics: Fourth Quarter 1979, 1980, No. 1; compiled in Dov Zakheim, "Of Allies and Access," The Washington Quarterly, Winter 1981.

[1]The following Persian Gulf states were included: Abu Dhabi, United Arab Emirates, Iran, Iraq, Kuwait, Qatar, Saudi Arabia.

2. Threats

Violent threats to assured Western access to Persian Gulf oil are sepa-
rable into three distinct categories: (1) *direct Soviet aggression* against
an oil-producing state, oil fields, or maritime oil supply routes in the
region; (2) *aggression by another regional power* against an oil-produc-
irtg state, field or routes; and (3) *terrorism, rebellion, or revolution* within
an oil-producing state. Military requirements for dealing effectively with
these threats differ widely, and in the case of internal challenges to an
oil-producing state the utility of U.S. military intervention becomes problematical; much depends on the amount of warning time and whether
intervention is requested by the threatened regime.

Direct Soviet Aggression

While the USSR has never forcibly conquered an oil-producing state,[4]
the Soviet invasion of Afghanistan in December 1979 demonstrated both
willingness and capacity to use military power directly against a country
in the greater Gulf region in a manner posing a distinct menace to Western
interests in the area. Given the steady deterioration of central authority in
neighboring Iran (exacerbated by the ongoing Iraqi-Iranian war) and a
history of unflagging imperial Russian designs on that country, the Soviet
occupation of Afghanistan complicates an already difficult Western defense of the Persian Gulf.

Whatever the motive underlying the Soviet decision to invade Afghanistan,[5] the establishment of a Soviet military presence in that country
poses a heightened threat to Western interests in the Gulf. A Soviet
Afghanistan almost doubles the length of Soviet controlled border with

---

[4]Some might cite the Soviet "liberation" of Rumania in 1944 as an exception. It should be
noted, however, that Rumania declared war on the Soviet Union in 1941 and that the
Rumanian army participated in the German invasion of Russia and in subsequent operations on the Eastern Front. Clearly, any Persian Gulf state that attacked the Soviet Union
could expect the same fate.

[5]Western analysts remain divided on the subject. Some regard the invasion as the product
of purely defensive considerations, and accordingly minimize its strategic consequences
for the West. Others view it as part of a larger offensive design on the region. For an
exploration of both points of view, see Patrick J. Garrity, "The Soviet Military Stake in
Afghanistan: 1956-1979," and Geoffrey Warhurst, "Afghanistan—A Dissenting Appraisal,"
Journal of the Royal United Services Institute for Defence Studies, September 1980.

Iran, brings Soviet forces some 300 miles closer to the realization of a centuries-old dream of a warm-water port in the Arabian Sea, and opens the lengthy and highly porous Afghani-Pakistan border to potential Soviet penetration. There have already been reports of Soviet attacks on Pakistani border posts, although such reports have been denied by the Soviet Union.

From a purely military standpoint the occupation of Afghanistan threatens an already tenuous balance in the region. Aside from an impressive demonstration that the Soviets have achieved an operational mastery of their burgeoning capacity to project military force abroad (at least into areas in close proximity to the USSR), the occupation extends the unrefueled reach of Soviet tactical airpower to areas—most notably, the Gulf of Oman and Strait of Hormuz—heretofore regarded as aerial sanctuaries by the United States. Coupled with the proliferation of Soviet naval bases, anchorages, and port facilities in the Red Sea, the Gulf of Aden, and the Persian Gulf itself (depicted in Map 1), the presence of Soviet airpower in Afghanistan confers upon the Kremlin the power to sever the West's economic jugular in the Gulf.[6]

Whether Soviet forces will advance beyond Afghanistan (into Iran or Pakistan) remains a matter of speculation. In Afghanistan Moscow obviously was deterred neither by Western military power in the region[7] nor by the prospect of indigenous resistance, although the stoutness and resiliency of the latter clearly was not anticipated.

On the other hand, the military and political price of conquering and occupying either Iran or Pakistan would be far greater than that which the Soviet Union has been forced to pay in Afghanistan. In area and population both countries are substantially larger than Afghanistan,[8] and both are resolutely Islamic in cultural and religious outlook. These factors suggest the prospect of a level of popular resistance to a Soviet invasion dwarfing that in Afghanistan. Another "Afghanistan" in Iran or Pakistan could in turn inflame the entire Islamic world against the Soviet Union.

---

[6]An excellent analysis of the Soviet naval challenge to Western sea lines of communication in the Gulf region is presented in Robert J. Hanks, *The Unnoticed Challenge: Soviet Maritime Strategy and the Global Choke Points* (Cambridge, MA: Institute for Foreign Policy Analysis, 1980).

[7]A direct Western defense of Afghanistan was militarily impossible, given the country's border with the Soviet Union and inaccessibility by sea.

[8]Afghanistan encompasses 250,000 square miles and almost 15 million people; Iran, 636,000 square miles and 38 million people; and Pakistan, 310,000 square miles and 83 million people.

MAP 1
The Indian Ocean and Persian Gulf: Western Oil Supply Routes and Areas of Soviet Influence

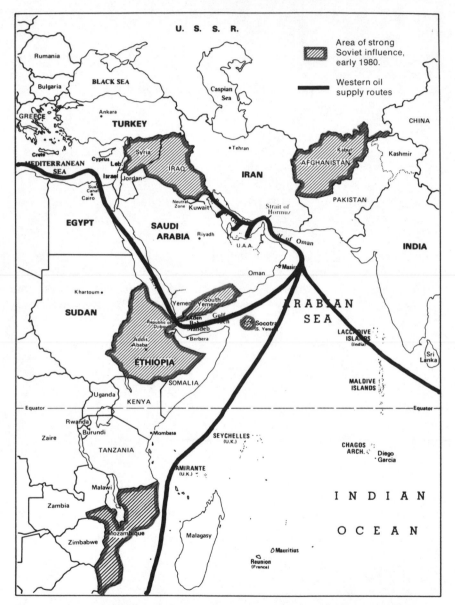

Source: Adapted from map appearing in John M. Collins, *U.S.-Soviet Military Balance: Concepts and Capabilities, 1960-1980* (New York: McGraw-Hill, 1980), p. 368.

The logistical problems involved in an attempt to incorporate Iran or Pakistan into the Soviet empire also would be more formidable than those encountered in Afghanistan. Soviet ground forces are separated from Iran's principal oil fields by several hundred miles of desert and rugged mountains; in the case of Pakistan, Soviet logistical support would have to be delivered through Afghanistan itself.

Logistical difficulties would multiply in any attempt to seize a country on the more distant Arabian peninsula. Soviet forces would be denied an overland approach, being compelled to rely instead on fragile air and sea lines of communication subject to interdiction by U.S. sea-based air power and other naval forces in the Indian Ocean. The success the Soviet Union has enjoyed to date in utilizing its airlift and sealift capabilities to supply its far-flung Cuban and other surrogate forces in the Third World has been attributable in no small way to the absence of any direct military challenge to those air and sea lines of communication. Slow and un-armed, strategic air transports are particularly easy game, especially when operating at distances beyond the radius of tactical fighter escorts.

In sum, while one cannot entirely dismiss the possibility of an "Afghani-stan" being visited upon an oil-producing state in the Gulf or of a Soviet attempt, for example, to block the Strait of Hormuz, it is likely that the price to the Kremlin of either venture would vastly exceed perceived benefits. The former would risk immersion in a military quagmire ap-proaching that of the United States in Indochina, whereas the latter would be tantamount to an act of war against the United States and the West as a whole.

A more likely prospect would be the lightning employment of limited Soviet military force to assist local pro-Soviet forces in seizing power within an oil-producing state or to preempt the arrival of U.S. forces in a crisis area. For such a purpose the Soviet Army's formidable airborne forces are especially well-suited; indeed, they formed the cutting edge of the surprise invasion of Afghanistan. Soviet airborne forces consist of some seven divisions, each containing 8,500 men and over 300 armored vehicles, and a fleet of transport aircraft sufficient to move the assault echelons of three divisions simultaneously.[9]

---

[9]C. Kenneth Allard, "A Clear and Present Danger: Soviet Airborne Forces in the 1980s," a paper presented before the Conference on Projection of Power: Perspectives, Perceptions, and Logistics, Ninth Annual Conference of the International Security Studies Program, The Fletcher School of Law and Diplomacy, Tufts University, Boston, Massachusetts, April 23-25, 1980.

Given the proximity of the Soviet Union to the Gulf, the inherent strategic mobility of airborne forces, and the Soviet military's pronounced doctrinal and operational emphasis on surprise, distant U.S. rapid deployment forces could well arrive in the Persian Gulf only to find their objectives already occupied by Soviet airborne forces which, unlike their U.S. counterparts, possess impressive firepower and a high level of tactical mobility. The choice at that point would be unenviable: to withdraw, or fire the first shot against the Soviet Union.

It is somewhat paradoxical that the Carter Doctrine and related pronouncements focus largely on deterrence of direct Soviet aggression in the Persian Gulf. The doctrine's inference that the United States would eschew resort to violence in the Gulf in circumstances not involving visible "outside force" is unfortunate, since, as we shall see, violence indigenous to the region—including Soviet-sponsored subversion—constitutes a far more pressing threat to assured U.S. access to Gulf oil than the unlikely prospect of a Soviet tank army crashing into the region. As then Under-Secretary of Defense Robert Komer conceded in 1980, following the Soviet invasion of Afghanistan, "the most immediate threat to stability in the Indian Ocean area is not an overt Russian attack but rather internal instability, coups, [and] subversion. . . ."[10]

In any event, the ability of the United States to mount a successful territorial defense of at least Iran and Pakistan against a determined Soviet invasion is questionable, given the size of Soviet ground and tactical air forces and their proximity to both those countries. In the author's judgment, if the Soviets are deterred from an invasion of Iran or Pakistan, they are deterred less by the prospect of an effective U.S. military response and more by the enormous political and military occupation costs either venture would entail.

A U.S. defense of Iran against a Soviet invasion, which has attracted the attention of RDF force planners, would be especially difficult. Even with the advantage of sufficient warning, at best U.S. military forces might be able to conduct a series of delaying actions in central Iran (along the Zagroz Mountains), and in so doing buy enough time to establish military enclaves along Iran's Gulf coast and in Khuzistan. The success of such a strategy, however, would be completely contingent upon a number of factors, none of them likely to materialize: (1) an Iranian willingness to

---

[10]*Department of Defense Authorization for Appropriations for Fiscal Year 1981, Hearings* before the Committee on Armed Services, United States Senate, 96th Congress, Second Session (1980), Part 1, p. 445. (Hereinafter cited as *Hearings.*)

permit timely U.S. entry into key ports and airfields; (2) a willingness on the part of Saudi Arabia, Oman, and other states on the Arabian peninsula to allow U.S. utilization of their territory for the purpose of defending Iran; (3) the ability of U.S. naval forces to prevent the interdiction of the Strait of Hormuz by Soviet submarines and Backfire bombers; and (4) the ability of the United States to confine the conflict to the Gulf region.

The last factor would be a major strategic imponderable in any U.S.-Soviet clash in the Gulf. It is difficult to imagine a sizable shooting war between the United States and the Soviet Union in the Gulf alone. In all probability the conflict would soon expand at least to the European theater. This raises the prospect of a war on two strategically independent fronts against an adversary possessing superior forces on both and enjoying the advantages of interior lines of communication between them. The problem is underlined by the decision to form the Rapid Deployment Force largely from units already committed to NATO.

Aggression by a Regional Power

Aggression against an oil-producing state by another Gulf country represents a second category of violent threats to U.S. interests in the Persian Gulf. Unlike direct Soviet aggression in the Gulf, this threat has already materialized in a dramatic fashion. The 1980 Iraqi invasion of Iran's oil-rich province of Khuzistan severely disrupted oil production in both countries; breaching an unwritten law of warfare in the Middle East, both sides employed tactical air power directly against each other's refineries and oil transport facilities.

More disturbing than the temporary disruption of oil production at the northern end of the Gulf has been the possible emergence of Iraq from the conflict as the preeminent military and economic power in the Gulf region, in firm possession of the critical Shatt-al-Arab waterway and possibly in control of a sizable segment of Iran's oil heartland.

Neither the repulsive character of the present Iranian government (whose attempts to subvert the Baathist regime in Baghdad contributed to the outbreak of the war) nor the justifiable anger within the United States over the seizure and retention of American hostages in Tehran should hobble pursuit of the central U.S. state interest in preventing any single power, especially a longstanding friend of the Soviet Union, from achieving dominance within the Gulf.

While not discounting the possibility of other local aggression in the Gulf region—for example, a South Yemeni attack on Oman—the possible rise of Iraq as the preponderant military power on the Arabian peninsula poses a distinct and militarily challenging potential threat to U.S. interests in the Gulf. Although Saudi Arabia and most other Gulf states have diplomatically supported Baghdad during the Iraqi-Iranian war, they have done so largely out of hatred of the Shiite regime in Tehran and fear that a neutralist stance would exacerbate longstanding political antagonisms between Iraq and the nonsocialist, conservative monarchical regimes to the south.

The prospect of an Iraqi attack on Kuwait or Saudi Arabia merits particular attention because (1) even before the Iraqi-Iranian war such a contingency exerted a major influence on U.S. force planning for non-NATO contingencies; (2) Iraq's Soviet-supplied armed forces are the largest of any in the Gulf region; and (3) the principal oil fields of Kuwait and Saudi Arabia are within comparatively easy reach from Iraq's southern border (see Map 2). Iraq is certainly no puppet of the Soviet Union; her foreign policy, however, has been distinctly hostile to the United States and, until recently, to Kuwait and Saudi Arabia.[11] (In 1961 Iraq attempted to conquer Kuwait, and was finally deterred only by British and Arab League forces.)

This hostility constitutes a potentially explosive factor in the region, given the comparative military weakness of Iraq's neighbors. As shown in Table 2, Iraq's active military forces, containing some 220,000 men, over 5,300 tanks and armored fighting vehicles (including Soviet T-62 main battle tanks and BMP infantry fighting vehicles), and 310 combat aircraft (among them, some 80 MiG-23Bs), exceed the *combined* military forces of Saudi Arabia, Oman, North and South Yemen, Qatar, Kuwait, and the United Arab Emirates. More significantly, as we shall see, the firepower and tactical mobility of Iraqi ground forces dwarf those of U.S. ground forces that could be rapidly brought to bear on the Arabian peninsula.

The performance of Iraqi forces admittedly has not been commensurate with potential capabilities. Iraqi military operations in 1967, 1973, and especially during the ongoing conflict with Iran have been characterized by sluggishness on the ground, misuse of tactical airpower, lack of imagination, and downright incompetence.[12] In relation to the inexperienced comic-opera military establishments of most potential adversaries on the Arabian peninsula, however, Iraqi forces do pose a serious threat.

It should go without saying that the employment of U.S. military power on behalf of a country threatened by Iraq (or any other state) would have to

---

[11]Iraq's foreign policy and military capabilities are cogently analyzed in Claudia Wright, "Iraq—New Power in the Middle East," *Foreign Affairs,* Winter 1979/1980.

[12]Abdul Kasim Mansur (pseudonym), "The Military Balance in the Persian Gulf: Who Will Guard the Gulf States from Their Guardians?," *Armed Forces Journal,* November 1980.

MAP 2
Persian Gulf Oil Fields

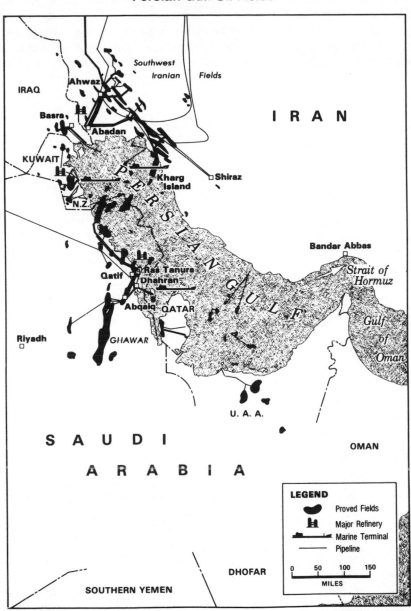

Source: John M. Collins, *U.S.-Soviet Military Balance: Concepts and Capabilities, 1960-1980* (New York: McGraw-Hill, 1980), p. 380.

be predicated on a positive request for assistance on the part of the threatened state. It is problematical, however, whether such a request would be made before the outbreak of hostilities: the pre-war arrival of U.S. combat forces on the soil of Kuwait or Saudi Arabia could compromise the political legitimacy of the host government in the eyes of its own people and within the Arab world as a whole, to say nothing of providing a pretext for the very invasion it was designed to deter. Regional sensitivity to a pre-war U.S. military presence, already evident in the refusal of Saudi Arabia and Oman to permit the stationing on their own territory of advanced detachments of the Rapid Deployment Force, poses significant military problems for any U.S. intervention force. It heightens the prospect that intervention would have to be conducted under fire, which places a premium on such expensive forcible-entry capabilities as amphibious assault shipping and naval gunfire support. It also suggests a probability that key terrain and high-value economic objectives would already be in the hands of enemy forces. As in the case of the lightning employment of Soviet airborne forces, the Rapid Deployment Force could again be preempted.

Terrorism, Rebellion, or Revolution within an Oil-Producing State

The fall of the Shah of Iran serves as a constant reminder that assured U.S. access to Persian Gulf oil can be endangered as much by events within an oil-producing state as by events from without. Indeed, the internal political fragility of oil-producing states, many of which consist of semi-feudal regimes governing disparate populations within the confines of boundaries all too often arbitrarily established by 19th-century European colonial offices,[13] may be regarded as the weakest single link in the chain of Western deterrence in the Persian Gulf. The vulnerability of such regimes to Soviet-sponsored subversion and to overthrow by purely indigenous forces of nationalism and religious fanaticism has been demonstrated in North and South Yemen, Iran, and in the bloody assault by a "false Mahdi" on Mecca's Grand Mosque in early 1980.

A principal feature of intra-national threats to U.S. interests in the Persian Gulf—and one of immense policy significance for the United States—is that terrorism, rebellion and revolution, supported or not by "outside

---

[13]Oil-rich Kuwait, formerly a British protectorate, is illustrative. Kuwaitis form less than one-half the population of the kingdom and only about 20 percent of its work force. The balance consists largely of Bedouin tribesmen, Arabs from other countries (including a large number of Palestinians), and foreigners, mostly Iranians, Indians, and Pakistanis. Political power is concentrated almost exclusively in the hands of the ruling Sabah dynasty.

16

forces," are far less susceptible to purely military solutions than the problems of direct Soviet aggression or local aggression against an oil-producing state. As the United States learned painfully in Vietnam, military intervention is likely to be self-defeating if it is conducted on behalf of a regime otherwise unable to maintain itself in the face of determined indigenous challenges to its authority.

Iran is no less a case in point. The unfolding debate in the United States over "who lost Iran" carries with it the suggestion that the triumph of nationalistic, Islamic fundamentalism in that country could have been thwarted from the Situation Room in the White House. The debate ignores the fact that the Shah's vulnerability to those forces stemmed in no small part from widening perceptions among his own people that, as a self-advertised client of the United States, he had allowed Iran to become the puppet of a "sinful," non-Islamic "imperial" power. To have committed U.S. military power in an attempt to save the Shah would have served only to reinforce those perceptions and invite another Vietnam.

Terrorism, rebellion, and revolution are ultimately rooted in poverty, official corruption, autocratic rule, excessively rapid economic development in a backward social and religious environment, gross maldistribution of wealth, inequitable ownership of land, and ethno-religious antagonisms—problems endemic throughout the Persian Gulf. Accordingly, the use of military power alone—and certainly foreign military power—in dealing with them may be regarded as irrelevant and even dangerous. Other valuable tools are available to the United States and its Western allies in the form of development aid, technical assistance, trade reform, and a diplomacy that quietly encourages political reform.

To sum up, the efficacy of military responses to the myriad threats confronting assured U.S. access to Persian Gulf oil varies widely according to the character of the threat in question. In some cases military intervention would be entirely inappropriate and even self-defeating, in others, it would be not just appropriate but critical. Even under the latter circumstances, however, effective intervention would have to surmount powerful political and military obstacles, a subject to which we now turn.

TABLE 2
The Military Balance on the Arabian Peninsula, 1980

	Iraq[1]	Kuwait	Saudi Arabia	Bahrain	Qatar	United Arab Emirates	Oman	South Yemen	North Yemen
Ground Forces									
Manpower	180,000	10,000	31,000	2,300	4,000	23,500	11,500	22,000	30,000
Tanks	2,700	280	380	none	24	none	none	375	864
AFVs[2]	2,600	250	600	109	68	200+	40+	220	498
Artillery[3]	2,300+	90+	?	negligible	10+	20+	40+	325+	625+
Air Forces									
Manpower	38,000	1,900	14,500	none	300	750	1,800	1,300	1,500
Combat aircraft	332	50	136	none	4	52	38	111	49
Helicopters	276	34	40	none	11	29	24	14+	15
Naval Forces									
Manpower	4,250	500	1,500	200	400	900	900	500	600
Vessels	72	46	86	23	35	15	19	22	10
Para-Military Forces									
Manpower	79,800	15,000	26,500	none	none	negligible	3,300	15,000	20,000

Source: Compiled from information provided in The Military Balance, 1980-1981 (London: International Institute for Strategic Studies, 1980), pp. 40-50.

[1] Order of battle prior to outbreak of Iraqi-Iranian War in September 1980.
[2] Includes light tanks and all other types of armored fighting vehicles except for self-propelled artillery.
[3] Includes air-defense systems and crew-served anti-tank systems.

3. Obstacles to and Requirements for Effective Military Intervention

Formidable although not insurmountable obstacles would confront any sizable U.S. military intervention in the Persian Gulf. Each imposes a corollary requirement for successful intervention. For analytical purposes the obstacles can be grouped into two categories: military and political. The former includes (1) distance, (2) the exacting character of natural and likely operational environments in the region, (3) the lack of assured bases or access to bases ashore, (4) the difficulty of defending oil fields, (5) the strategic risk intrinsic in reliance on intervention forces that are for the most part already committed to the defense of areas outside the Gulf region, and (6) the pervasive material and operational unreadiness of U.S. general purpose forces, especially ground forces. The chief political obstacle to effective intervention is the absence of politically reliable and militarily competent U.S. client states in the region, whose assistance might prove vital in a major contingency.

Overshadowing all of these impediments is the heavy burden of a declining U.S. military reputation which, by raising the question of *American* military competence, has served to encourage adversaries and discourage potential allies.

Distance

No area of the world is more distant from the United States than the Persian Gulf. Airline distances from the east coast of the United States to the Gulf exceed 7,000 nautical miles. By sea, over which most of the currently-planned U.S. Rapid Deployment Force would be compelled to move, distances range from 8,500 nautical miles via the Suez Canal to 12,000 nautical miles via the Cape of Good Hope.

The military significance of these distances for the United States is a function of three factors. First, most of the military units currently earmarked for rapid deployment are stationed in the United States, requiring an enormous investment in means of moving them quickly to the Persian Gulf. Second, the United States possesses virtually no military bases in the region, imposing unusually demanding logistical requirements for sustaining forces once deployed to the Gulf. Third, Soviet forces available for combat in the region, as well as Iraqi and other Soviet-model armies, are far larger and much closer to the Gulf than U.S. forces;[14] the condemnation of at least early arriving RDF forces to almost certain numerical inferiority places a premium on superior operational and tactical employment of the RDF, and on seeking to ensure the RDF's arrival at the point of dispute *before* hostilities begin. Achieving the latter, of course, demands intelligence capabilities sufficient to provide ample warning of intended aggression in the region. It also requires a willingness on the part of political decision-makers to deploy U.S. forces to a crisis spot under circumstances likely to be characterized by ambiguity with regard to the immediacy of the threat and understandable concern that preemptive deployment could provoke the very outbreak of violence it was designed to deter.

The adverse operational consequences of the Gulf's logistical remoteness would be compounded in contingencies requiring the commitment of substantial ground forces ashore. Strong surface naval forces can be maintained indefinitely (although at great cost) in the region, as they are today. Land-based tactical air forces can be moved quickly from the United States to the Gulf, if provided adequate aerial tanker support (which requires access to air installations en route) and assured reception at terminal facilities in the Gulf. Sizable ground forces, however, especially armored and mechanized formations, cannot be moved quickly by air or by sea, as shown in Table 3. A minimum of 50 days would be needed to "close"[15] a complete mechanized division to the Gulf, utilizing the full resources of the U.S. Military Airlift Command; some 21 days would be required to deploy even the 82nd Airborne Division, the smallest division in the U.S. Army. Sealift, the only real means of moving large ground forces, also would entail substantial time in transit, especially if compelled to enter the Indian Ocean via the Cape of Good Hope. Even U.S. Marine amphibious forces already deployed in the Western Pacific would need 12-14 days after embarkation to reach objectives inside the Persian Gulf.[16]

---

[14] According to the International Institute for Strategic Studies, Soviet ground forces in the North Caucasus, Trans-Caucasus, and Turkestan military districts consist of some 24 divisions. An additional 5-6 divisions have been deployed to Afghanistan. *The Military Balance, 1980-1981* (London: International Institute for Strategic Studies, 1980), pp. 10-11.

[15] "Closure" is Pentagon jargon for the time needed to move a unit *in its entirety* from the United States to some point overseas. In cases involving reliance on airlift, the first elements of a unit would arrive well in advance of the unit's closure time, as shown in Table 3.

[16] John M. Collins, *U.S.-Soviet Military Balance: Concepts and Capabilities, 1960-1980* (New York: McGraw-Hill, 1980), p. 387.

TABLE 3
Estimated Closure Times to the Persian Gulf of U.S.-Based Ground Forces

Type of Force	Mode of Movement	Total Weight (in tons)	Personnel[1]	Arrival of First Element	Closure[2]
				Times (in days)	
Airborne Brigade	air	11,900	4,000	2	6
Airborne Division	air	52,400	27,500	2	21
Mechanized Brigade	air	34,300	7,900	2	16
	sea	34,300	7,900	—	9
Mechanized Division	air	120,200	32,300	2	50
	sea	120,200	32,300	26	37
Armored Brigade	air	31,700	7,200	2	13
	sea	31,700	7,200	24	26
Armored Division	air	110,500	31,800	2	48
	sea	110,500	31,800	24	36

Source: Information provided to the author by sources in the Department of Defense.

[1] Includes combat service and combat service support personnel associated with unit.
[2] The day on which the last remaining element of the unit arrives.

Although realization of Department of Defense strategic lift enhancement and maritime prepositioning programs (discussed in detail in Chapter 4) will increase the pace at which the United States could "close" military forces to the Persian Gulf, the programs offer no solution to the prospect of preemption by Soviet airborne forces, whose strategic mobility is calculable in hours and days rather than weeks.

The inherent difficulties of sustaining airborne forces that are isolated from friendly contact on the ground and dependent on aerial resupply has been demonstrated repeatedly since the birth of airborne warfare in the 1940s.[17] Yet the deterrent value of a preemptive deployment of Soviet airborne forces in a U.S.-Soviet confrontation in the Persian Gulf region should not be underestimated. While militarily feasible, attacking either Soviet airborne forces already in place on the ground or their air lines of communication would require a degree of political resolve and willingness to take risks uncharacteristic of U.S. foreign policy since Vietnam. Indeed, it has been argued that success in such a confrontation would crown not the side that got there "fustest with the mostest" but the side that simply got there first with any measurable force.

The United States does not have ground forces stationed on the territory that would be threatened, and geography favors the Soviets in a countdown toward competitive intervention. *The Middle East is an area in which preemption is the only reasonable strategy for either of the superpowers;* preemption not in terms of strikes against each other's forces, but in terms of reaching the scene first. Once one of the superpowers' troops are on the disputed ground, counterintervention becomes a much more reckless venture for the other, because he then has the "last clear chance" to avoid the dangers inherent in undertaking the unprecedented action of combat between two nuclear-armed states. The danger of surprise here, for the United States, is not so much the edge it can give as a force multiplier in determining the outcome of battle; rather it is the danger that by being slow on the draw, Washington may be deterred from any direct engagement at all.[18]

Exacting Natural and Operational Combat Environments

A second obstacle to successful U.S. military intervention in the Persian Gulf region is the rigorous natural and likely combat environments in which U.S. forces would be compelled to fight in the region. Allegiance

---

[17]The fate of the British 1st Airborne Division at Arnhem in 1944 is a monument to the fragility of large-scale airborne operations in hostile territory.

[18]Richard K. Betts, *Surprise and Defense: The Lesson of Sudden Attacks for U.S. Military Planning,* a draft manuscript scheduled for publication by the Brookings Institution in 1981, p. IX-10.

to a strategy of preemption, the desirability of which is recognized by RDF force planners, does not diminish the need for powerful intervention forces. The preemptive arrival of a small U.S. force at the disputed point would not preclude it from being attacked or overrun by larger hostile forces arriving subsequently on the scene, including forces of a regional power. Getting U.S. forces to the Gulf in a timely fashion is only part of the problem; upon arrival, those forces must be capable of conducting successful operations in rugged, waterless terrain, and in all probability against numerically superior and fully mechanized opponents possessing substantial firepower and a high degree of tactical mobility.

Desert warfare is one of the most logistically demanding of combat environments. The combination of heat and sand places extraordinary demands on the maintenance of all forms of equipment, from rifles to main battle tanks and aircraft (helicopters are especially prone to breakdown, as the United States discovered in the Iranian desert in April 1980). Additionally, the barrenness of the desert requires complete self-sufficiency even in such common essentials as water. Indeed, the requirement for water alone is astounding; Rapid Deployment Joint Task Force planners have calculated that a minimum of 12 gallons of water (weighing 100.2 pounds and encompassing 1.6 cubic feet) per man per day would be required to sustain a force on the Arabian peninsula.[19]

Of significance is the fact that the U.S. military has had little experience in desert warfare, and none at all since Axis forces were driven from North Africa in 1943. This inexperience is manifest in the dearth within service inventories of such critical items as water desalination, well-drilling, and water storage equipment.[20]

No less demanding than the natural environment of the Arabian peninsula is the likely operational environment, especially in contingencies involving combat against Soviet or Soviet-model forces. The problem can be simply stated: *Rapidly deployable U.S. ground forces are least suited for combat in the Persian Gulf; conversely, ground forces that are most suitable are not rapidly deployable.*[21] Like most modern countries, the United States maintains two basic types of ground forces: heavy forces, consisting of tank and mechanized infantry formations; and light forces,

---

[19]John K. Cooley, "US Rapid Strike Force: How to Get There First with the Most," *Christian Science Monitor,* April 11, 1980; and George C. Wilson, "Supplying Water: The Big Hurdle for Desert Force," *Washington Post,* October 10, 1980.

[20]John J. Fialka, "Rapid Deployment Meaningless Without Fuel, Water," *Washington Star,* April 9, 1980.

[21]See, for example, Jeffrey Record, "Why Plan Rapid Deployment of the Wrong Kind of Force?," *Washington Star,* February 3, 1980.

composed of airborne, amphibious, "straight-legged" infantry, and other foot-mobile units.

Heavy forces are organized around tanks, armored personnel carriers and self-propelled artillery. They possess great firepower and are extremely mobile on the battlefield, since they move entirely on tracked or wheeled vehicles. Heavy forces are best suited for combat against other heavy forces on flat, rolling, and comparatively unobstructed terrain. It is for these reasons that most of the U.S. Army's heavy divisions are deployed in Europe or earmarked for NATO contingencies.

Light U.S. ground forces, which include the Marine Corps' three divisions, are structured primarily for combat outside Europe, particularly in areas where the use of armor is inhibited either by the potential adversary's lack of armor or by terrain (jungles, forests, mountains, etc.). Because light forces lack the firepower of heavy formations and depend mainly on marching for moving around on the battlefield, they do not hold up well in combat against heavy formations. This is especially the case in terrain, such as deserts, tailor-made for high-speed armored operations of the type that have characterized much of warfare in the Middle East during the past 20 years.

Light forces, however, do possess one distinct advantage over heavy forces: precisely because they are light, they can be moved quickly from one region of the world to another. The very thing that makes light forces relatively immobile on the battlefield—the comparative lack of tanks and other heavy armored fighting vehicles—makes them easier to transport from the United States to a potential battlefield overseas. In contrast, as noted, heavy forces possess little strategic mobility.

And it is here that we confront the great paradox of the Rapid Deployment Force: Those U.S. ground forces most rapidly deployable overseas are least suited for combat against potential U.S. adversaries in the Middle East and South Asia. The days are long gone when a handful of Western troops armed with a few Maxim guns could awe and subdue the non-industrialized regions of the world. As noted, future contingencies in the Middle East are likely to involve combat against numerically superior Soviet-model client armies of heavy forces whose tactical mobility and firepower, even battalion for battalion, far exceed that now possessed by either U.S. Army or Marine light forces. As also noted, the Iraqi Army alone fields some 5,300 tanks and armored fighting vehicles, almost twelve times the Marine Corps' entire inventory; the Syrian Army has some 2,600 tanks; even the tiny army of South Yemen has 375, seven times that of an unmechanized U.S. Army infantry division.

Even Soviet airborne forces might prove more than a match for early-arriving RDF contingents, should the decision be made to attack them. In a seminal article published in the *Armed Forces Journal* in January 1980, retired Army and Marine Corps generals James F. Hollingsworth and Allan T. Wood concluded:

The US does have airmobile forces. Our Marine divisions and Army strike forces give us some of this capability, but a total comparative evaluation shows us to be sadly lacking. Third World forces in many areas of the world are now equipped with thousands of tanks. The Russians maintain complete airborne divisions with thousands of light armored vehicles. They have aircraft capable of rapidly deploying these divisions with their armor.

The Soviet Army now has at least seven airborne divisions available for deployment anywhere in the world. The Soviet airborne division is quite different from its US counterpart—it is, in fact, a light mechanized division with 346 BMDs. The BMD weighs 9 metric tons, about the same size as the US M-113 armored personnel carrier; however, it has considerably better combat capability. It mounts the same turret as the better known BMP.

The turret has an automatically loaded 73 mm smooth bore cannon and a Sagger missile mounted on top of the gun. The vehicle is lightly armored to provide protection against small arms and artillery fragments and is designed for the assault with machine guns located in the right and left front of the vehicle. In addition to the driver and squad leader, six paratroopers are carried in the troop compartment.

To round out the mobile combined arms team are nine ASU-57 tracked assault guns single lift on a short to medium range mission.

U.S. forces that could be delivered by air today are limited to the 101st Airborne, 82nd Airborne and several Marine divisions. Numerically, their personnel may equal the seven Russian airmobile divisions, but here the equality ends. The Russians have over 2,000 armored vehicles in their force—we have less than 200. Our medium tanks, such as the M-60 and XM-1, can be lifted only by the C-5A, which itself is available only in very limited numbers. Neither tank can be carried in a C-141. Our mechanized divisions cannot be transported overseas within a matter of weeks, let alone days or hours.

The process can take months by sea. What must be accomplished in the immediate future is to create a light armored corps with thousands of light armored vehicles that can be transported in existing aircraft.

Consider a Middle East scenario in which four U.S. divisions move against seven Soviet airborne divisions. Manpower-wise, the forces are approximately even; however, these divisions are woefully short of combat vehicles. This problem has been known for a long time, after repeated deployment in the REFORGER exercises in Europe. Brigades from the 82nd Airborne Division have been deployed to Europe for the past several years, but the critiques of these exercises have indicated that these brigades are good for a "one night stand" like the one fought by General Custer against the Indians at Little Big Horn: the enemy overwhelms the dismounted U.S. forces in tactical mobility and firepower. Foot mobility is simply not adequate to cope with the mechanized mobility of Soviet forces.[22]

The superiority of mechanized over unmechanized infantry in open terrain has long been recognized.

Non-motorized infantry divisions are only of value against a motorized and armored enemy when occupying prepared positions. If these positions are pierced or outflanked, a withdrawal will leave them helpless victims of a motorized enemy, with nothing else to do but surrender or hold on in their positions to the last round.[23]

In short, the kind of ground forces the United States might be able to deploy rapidly to the Middle East would face the prospect of swift destruction by quantitatively and qualitatively superior forces operating in terrain and a combat environment permitting the full exploitation of the weaknesses of foot-mobile infantry in the face of tanks.

Thus, if the United States is to develop a capacity for effective intervention on the ground in the "arc of crisis," more is required than simply the ability to move existing U.S. ground forces faster to that region. Staying on the battlefield is just as important as getting to it in time. What is needed is not just an increase in the strategic mobility of our present ground forces, but a new type of ground force combining the strategic mobility of light infantry and the tactical mobility and firepower of heavy ground forces.

Lack of Bases or of Assured Access to Bases

The unsuitability for Middle East combat of U.S. forces slated for intervention is compounded by a dearth of U.S. military bases in the Gulf region, making it impossible to sustain any major force presence ashore for an extended period of time. The criticality of bases was recently noted by Marine Lieutenant General Paul X. Kelley, commander of the Rapid Deployment Joint Task Force:

When you talk about projecting combat power 7,000 miles and then sustaining it over the long haul, it boggles the mind. That's why it's absolutely essential that we have access to facilities in the region.[24]

---

[22]"The Light Armored Corps—A Strategic Necessity," *Armed Forces Journal*, January 1980. A similar analysis may be found in Juan Cameron, "Our What—If Strategy for Mideast Trouble Spots," *Fortune*, May 7, 1979.

[23]Erwin Rommel, in B. H. Liddell Hart, editor, *The Rommel Papers* (New York: Harcourt, Brace and Company, 1953), p. 198.

[24]"Preserving the Oil Flow," *Time*, September 22, 1980, p. 29.

Kelley's views were echoed by the Department of Defense:

In order to support forward deployed forces better and introduce the RDF faster, it is imperative that facilities in the region be made available for U.S. use. Logistic support is crucial to the success of military operations. Unfortunately, in the Indian Ocean, the U.S. lacks the logistic facilities needed to support operations, especially during crises. Access to regional air- and port-reception facilities, storage facilities, . . . and assured host nation support help to overcome this shortfall.[25]

The projection of U.S. military power overseas has always required a network of secure refueling, resupply, and maintenance facilities on the fringes of the disputed region—a network which, without exception, has been based *on land*. The Normandy invasion of 1944 would have been impossible without prior military access to Great Britain; in the Pacific theater, Australia formed the logistical bedrock for MacArthur's reconquest of the Solomons, New Guinea, and the Philippines. Similarly, U.S. military operations on the Korean peninsula were critically dependent upon access to Japan; and in Vietnam, the United States enjoyed not only a network of installations ashore but also major facilities in the Philippines and Thailand.

These conditions do not apply in the Persian Gulf. Indeed, as stressed by the Department of Defense, with the exception of the tiny atoll of Diego Garcia, some 2,500 miles from the Strait of Hormuz, the United States possesses no military bases in that vast area of the world stretching from Turkey to the Philippines. (In contrast are the large Soviet installations at Cam Ranh, Socotra, and Aden, and longstanding Soviet access to the Iraqi bases at Umm Qasr and Al Basrah.) Nor are prospects favorable for the establishment of a "Subic" naval facility or "Clark" air force base in the region. As confirmed by former Under-Secretary of Defense Komer, "the countries [in the area] . . . most emphatically do not want formal security arrangements with us."[26]

The political sensitivity of potential host nations to a permanent U.S. military presence on their own soil is certainly understandable. Such a presence "would validate the criticisms of radical Arabs about how the conservative [Gulf] states are toadies of the imperialists," and thus "increase the chances of the internal turmoil that constitutes the main potential threat."[27]

---

[25]*Hearings, op. cit.,* p. 484.

[26]*Ibid.,* p. 445.

[27]Betts, *op. cit.,* p. IX-14. See also Abdul Kasim Mansur (pseudonym), "The American Threat to Saudi Arabia," *Armed Forces Journal,* September 1980; Richard F. Grimmett, *Prospective American Use of Foreign Bases for Military Action Against Iran* (Washington, D.C.: Congressional Research Service, December 10, 1979); and Norman Kempster, "Keep Low Persian Gulf Profile, Saudi Urges U.S,," *Los Angeles Times,* September 20, 1979.

Moreover, many Gulf states continue to regard U.S. support for Israel as a greater threat to the security of the Arab world than the prospect of an "Afghanistan" on the Arabian peninsula. Some even suspect the United States of coveting the peninsula's oil fields, a suspicion reflected in the following statement of Sheik Sabah al Ahmad al Sabah, Kuwait's Foreign Minister:

Defend us against whom? Who's occupying us? We haven't asked anybody to defend us. Yet we find all these ships around asking for facilities. It's all a bit like a film with two directors—Russia and the U.S. How will the film end? Perhaps with both big powers agreeing, "O.K., these oil fields belong to us, and those to you. We'll divide up the region from here to there." Is that how it will end?[28]

The role of Israel in the foreign policy calculus of many Gulf states was vividly summed up by Saudi Foreign Minister Prince Saud:

Israeli aggression is no better than Soviet aggression. If the U.S. wants to bring stability and protect independence in this region, then how can it ask our cooperation in opposing the Soviet occupation of Afghanistan unless it also opposes Israeli occupation of the Palestinian lands occupied in 1967?[29]

To its credit, the Department of Defense appears acutely cognizant of the political barriers to establishing a permanent U.S. military presence ashore in the Gulf region, and accordingly has pursued the alternative of gaining contingent rights of access to selected facilities in time of crisis. Successful negotiations along these lines have been concluded with Kenya, Somalia, and Oman. (See Chapter 4.)[30]

Unfortunately, as we shall see, simply having the promise of access to facilities on a contingency basis is no substitute for U.S.-controlled and -operated bases whose use is not subject to momentary political calculations of host governments. The same internal political considerations that deny the United States a permanent military presence ashore in the region could well be invoked to deny the United States access to facilities in the event of a crisis, irrespective of the agreements that have been negotiated. As a senior advisor to the Sultan of Oman pointedly reminded the Carter Administration, "The U.S. must have access to our facilities, but only on request. It is up to us to say yes or no."[31]

In short, any shore-based logistical infrastructure designed to support U.S. military intervention on the ground in the Persian Gulf would rest upon the shifting political sands of what Henry Kissinger has aptly char-

---

[28]*Time, op. cit.,* p. 29.

[29]*Ibid.,* p. 29.

[30]The Carter Administration apparently rejected alleged Israeli offers of permanent bases in the Sinai. The fine French port of Djibouti also appears to be off limits. See Collins, *op. cit.,* p. 376.

[31]*Time, op. cit.,* p. 29.

acterized as "probably the most volatile, unstable and crisis-prone region of the world."[32] It is worth recalling that during the October War of 1973, the United States was denied overflight rights by *NATO* allies, countries usually regarded as more reliable than non-treaty U.S. "friends" in the Gulf.

Flights originating in West Germany were routed to Lajes (in the Azores) then through the Mediterranean area to Lod Airport (in Israel). This zigzagging route was used because the United States could not obtain diplomatic clearance to use bases, which MAC (the Military Airlift Command) usually used, in the United Kingdom, Spain, Italy, Greece, and Turkey. Also, the aircraft had to avoid over-flying land masses and had to stay out of airspace controlled by Arab countries.[33]

Access even to bases along the periphery of the Gulf region is not assured. For example, even though the Congress has lifted its ill-considered arms embargo of Turkey, there is no guarantee that the United States would be permitted to use its extensive air facilities in that country, critical though they might be to prosecution of hostilities against Soviet or Iraqi forces in a Gulf war. In a conflict that did not directly threaten Turkish security interests, U.S. utilization of the territory of a NATO ally as a base for the launching of air strikes and other combat operations would risk involving that ally in hostilities, thereby risking expansion of the war into a NATO-Warsaw Pact confrontation. In the 1973 conflict, Turkey denied the United States use of its bases in that country.

Indefensibility of Oil Fields

The difficulty of defending oil fields and oil shipping routes inside the Gulf against direct assault by terrorist or regular armed forces constitutes another obstacle to successful U.S. military intervention in the Persian Gulf. The spatial vastness of the Gulf's major oil fields (see Map 2, p. 15); the exposed nature of wells, pipelines, pumping stations, storage tanks, refineries, and loading piers (depicted in Figure 1, p. 32); and the vul-nerability of large, slow-moving, and unarmed tankers to aerial attack, artillery fire, and even small, hand-held rocket launchers[34]—all dictate a

---

[32]*Ibid.*, p. 28.

[33]*Airlift Operations of the Military Airlift Command During the 1973 Middle East War,* Report to the Congress (Washington, D.C.: Comptroller General of the United States, April 16, 1975), p. 9.

[34]The main shipping channel in the Strait of Hormuz is within artillery range of both Oman and Iran. The destruction of a single tanker in the Strait in all likelihood would be sufficient to interdict the flow of oil from the Gulf; ship owners (to say nothing of captains and crews) would hardly be eager to attempt "running" the Strait after such an incident, nor would maritime insurance companies be willing to guarantee against losses except at exorbitant rates. The chilling effect on insurance rates and on the level of tanker traffic of even *unfulfilled* threats to attack shipping in the Strait was vividly demonstrated following Iran's threat to do so shortly after the outbreak of the Iraqi-Iranian war in September 1980.

reliance on means other than the direct employment of military force to protect oil fields and facilities.

For the United States, the difficulties either of seizing oil fields intact or of restoring demolished fields would be virtually insurmountable.

Assault Requirements. Parachute and/or amphibious operations would not be necessary if a friendly country requesting U.S. support retained control of ports and airfields. Difficulties, however, would more than double if we had to crack defenses while simultaneously seizing and securing oil installations undamaged.

U.S. parachute assault troops, for example, are too few to cover obligatory objectives, even if surprise were possible. Shipping shortfalls make amphibious forces too slow. Saboteurs could wreak havoc before they steamed into sight, unless prior warning allowed ample time to preposition troops and equipment near proposed operational areas. Still, two factors might work in U.S. favor. Owners would likely defer destroying their own installations until the last minute. Implementing programs would be prolonged, even if plans were perfect and complete.

Small U.S. failures, however, would be costly. We would forfeit more than a million barrels of crude petroleum daily if sappers plugged just 100 wells. Production would suffer severely if enemy explosives experts struck sensitive, highly pressurized paraphernalia associated with gas-oil separators, stabilizers, and refineries.

Air cover and close air support would be needed to suppress enemy interceptor aircraft, surface-to-air missiles (SAMs), antiaircraft artillery, and defensive ground forces during any U.S. assault. The closest non-Arab land bases that U.S. Air Force fighters might use are in Israel, 1,000 miles west. Fliers with the Sixth Fleet are even further away. The Persian Gulf is a poor cockpit for U.S. carriers, according to Navy planners. Floating arsenals from PACOM [Pacific Command] likely would remain in the Gulf of Oman or Arabian Sea, well removed from assault waves they seek to support, if Soviet air power represented a threat. Attack aircraft could increase combat radii by trading ordnance for fuel, but loiter times over targets would not be long, unless they replenished supplies from tankers in flight.

Vertical/Short Takeoff and Landing (VTOL/VSTOL) aircraft, which could take up some slack, are in short supply. The seizure and/or construction of on-site bases, including expeditionary airfields with optical landing aids, arresting gear, and lights, thus would likely assume a high priority during early stages of any such operation.

Restoration Requirements. Military forces needed to seize and secure a lodgment on Persian Gulf shores could cope with cratered airfield runways and ruined port facilities, but could neither restore petroleum installations nor operate the system. Highly skilled civilian manpower and special materials would be required for such purposes. Several problems thus could be pronounced.

Successful saboteurs could impede, or perhaps even stop, the flow of oil at its source in the fields, at pipe-line choke points, at terminal facilities, or after products have been pumped aboard tankers.

Destroying wells would be counterproductive if a settlement were reached quickly. Rejuvenation times would be long. Attacks on ancillary installations, however, could cripple local oil industries without endangering basic resources. Terminals, for example, include a range of lucrative targets: tanks, pumps, pipes, piers—all in a compact complex. Power supplies are very susceptible to sabotage. Saudi Arabia's machinery presents special problems, generally being the biggest in the world: the biggest gas separators (50 of them); the biggest pumping stations (2 million barrels each per day); the biggest water-injection plants (400 million cubic feet daily from Abqaiq field alone); the biggest storage tanks, the biggest oil port, and the biggest desalinization plant (except for one in Kuwait). One-of-a-kind items like that would be time consuming and expensive to replace.

One well-blown pumping station, for example, could shut down a pipeline for 90 days (an explosion at Abqaiq on May 11, 1977 cost $100 million to repair). Professional demolition men could tear great gaps in collection capabilities where many pipes run in parallel. So could a few big bombs, properly placed.

Fire in an oilfield, tank-farm, or refinery can be fearsome. Light oils mixed with volatile materials are easy to ignite and hard to extinguish. Separators and stabilizers are especially flammable. A big fire in Kuwait's Burgen field burned for two months before being capped in summer 1978. Burning oil from offshore platforms, swept south by prevailing Persian Gulf winds, could block beaches and port facilities needed by U.S. assault forces. (The blowout at Ixtoc 1, 50 miles off Mexico's coast in the Bay of Campeche, burned from June 3, 1979 until March 24, 1980, when it eventually was smothered.) Finally, explosions in loading areas could level installations ashore. Just one supertanker carrying liquified natural gas or a chemical such as naphtha would suffice, if set on fire at pierside.

Restoration requirements would exceed U.S. capabilities, unless damage was quite restricted.

Sixteen private companies and three Government agencies once committed 650 men, two fire barges, five mobile drilling rigs, two "jack-up" rigs, 11 mud barges, a derrick barge with 500-ton crane, and a shore-based control center complete with communications, power sources, fuel supply, helipad, seaplane dock, and living quarters just to combat a single platform fire in the United States. Conflagration at just a few counterparts in the Persian Gulf would cause intractable problems.[35]

---

[35]Collins, *op. cit.,* pp. 391-392.

FIGURE 1
Schematic Diagram, Oil Fields and Facilities

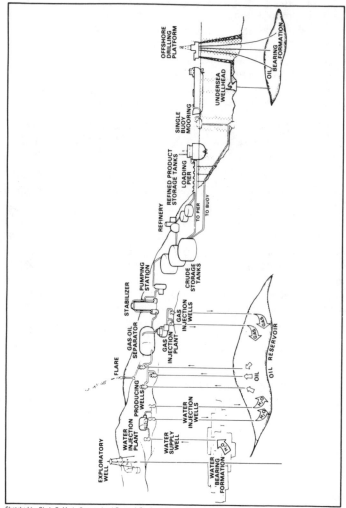

Sketched by Clyde R. Mark, Congressional Research Service, Library of Congress.

Source: John M. Collins, *U.S.-Soviet Military Balance: Concepts and Capabilities, 1960-1980* (New York: McGraw-Hill, 1980), p. 381.

Reliance on Dual-Committed Forces

A fifth obstacle to U.S. military intervention in the Persian Gulf is that it could be undertaken only at the price of diminished deterrence in Europe and the Far East. This inherent strategic risk of intervention could have been minimized had the vast new set of military requirements imposed on the United States by the Carter Doctrine been accompanied by commensurate increases in U.S. force levels. Unfortunately, requests for expanded force levels sufficient to mount a credible defense of U.S. interests in the Gulf without seriously degrading U.S. defense commitments elsewhere were not forthcoming from the Administration.

The decision to form the Rapid Deployment Force from existing military units (discussed in Chapter 4), most of which are already earmarked for NATO and the Far East, serves to widen what, even before Afghanistan, was a substantial gap between U.S. commitments abroad and capabilities to defend them. The decision makes it virtually impossible to deal effectively with a significant military challenge in more than one area at a time. As noted last year by William Perry, then Under-Secretary of Defense for Research and Development, "the really troublesome problem we have is how do we accommodate [a] NATO buildup and the Persian Gulf buildup at the same time? That is the rub."[36] Army Chief of Staff Edward C. Meyer has stated flatly that present U.S. force levels are "not sufficient to repel a Soviet assault [in the Persian Gulf] without jeopardizing our NATO commitment."[37] Chief of Naval Operations Thomas B. Hayward has testified that the present "1½ ocean Navy" of the United States cannot meet the "three-ocean commitment" imposed by the Carter Doctrine.[38]

Although U.S. military planning since 1969 has called for capabilities adequate to wage simultaneously a major conflict in Europe and a lesser conflict elsewhere (the so-called "1½-war" strategy), the simple truth is that U.S. force levels, now lower than at any point since the Korean War,[39]

---

[36]*Hearings, op. cit.,* Part 6, p. 3275.

[37]*Ibid,* Part 2, p. 745.

[38]*Ibid,* Part 2, p. 785.

[39]A benchmark year widely used for comparison with the present is 1964, the last year preceding the U.S buildup in Vietnam. For example, in 1964 personnel assigned to the active armed forces totaled 2.685 million compared to 2.059 million in fiscal year 1981; the active U.S. fleet contained 803 vessels compared to the present 430; the U.S. Air Force fielded a total of 439 active squadrons of all types compared to 253 today; and strategic sealift vessels numbered 100 compared to the present 48. In 1964 the United States allocated 8.4 percent of its gross national product to defense compared to less than 5 percent in the fiscal years 1977-1980.

are not sufficient to meet the demands of more than one sizable conflict at a time. The "½-war" in Vietnam was waged in no small part by U.S. forces earmarked for European contingencies. Similarly, the deployment in early 1980 of U.S. carrier battle groups in the Arabian Sea was made at the expense of carriers maintained on station along NATO's Southern Flank and in the Western Pacific.

Indeed, even planned increases in the size of the U.S. Fleet and in other critical power projection capabilities are unlikely to be adequate. A total of 97 ships were requested in the Carter Administration's Fiscal Year 1981 Defense Budget and Five-Year Defense Plan. Together with those vessels authorized in preceding years but not yet completed, the Plan will generate an active U.S. fleet of approximately 550 ships by the latter half of the 1980s. No net increase is planned in the present level (63 vessels) of amphibious shipping, which is a vital component of U.S. capability to project power ashore in a hostile environment. In Admiral Hayward's judgment, the shipbuilding program of the 1981 Five-Year Plan "represents a calculated risk . . . probably adequate to prevent further erosion of our relative posture," but not sufficient to fulfill the "obvious three ocean requirement."[40]

It is moreover highly doubtful whether the U.S. Navy, under the current All-Volunteer Force, is capable of manning a 550-ship fleet; existing shortfalls in skilled personnel are so severe that comparatively new vessels have been retired from active patrolling. As Admiral Hayward has cautioned,

It is important to remember that while looking at a new shipbuilding program and its importance to our future posture, and while looking at the possibility of bringing out ships that have been retired, that they must be manned by people. These people have to be talented and skilled. The major problem facing the Navy today, my highest priority, has to do with the retention of talented, skilled, trained manpower. It is a fundamental fact that all of our efforts to design and bring in new ships will go for naught if we do not retain skilled manpower in the right numbers. We are not doing so today.[41]

The strategic risk inherent in reliance on forces committed to both Gulf and non-Gulf contingencies would be profound in circumstances involving a U.S.-Soviet confrontation. By virtue of interior lines of communication, larger forces, and greater proximity to both Europe and the Gulf, the Soviet Union could, by feinting in one area, divert rapidly deployable U.S. forces away from the true point of decision.

---

[40]Hearings, op. cit., Part 2, pp. 913-914.

[41]Ibid., Part 2, p. 1050.

The U.S. defense establishment currently lacks much latitude to cope with sizable contingencies [in the Persian Gulf]. The Soviet side, whose large forces afford more flexibility, could sponsor several widely-separated hot spots at the same time, with assistance from allies and friends.

Possible application of U.S. military sinew to ensure petroleum imports from the Persian Gulf should be viewed in that perspective.

Our active status strategic reserves are too few to fight even a modest war in the Middle East without accepting calculated risks that uncover crucial interests elsewhere. Even "best case" forces would probably prove insufficient against the Soviets, whose abilities to project offensive power beyond their frontiers have improved impressively in recent years.[42]

This is not to suggest that present U.S. forces could be no better postured than they are today. On the contrary, the readiness, structure, weaponry, and logistical sustainability of many units are not optimized for many conceivable contingencies in the Gulf region. More fundamental is the comparatively small amount of real combat power generated by the present structure of U.S. military forces. The product in large part of low "tooth-to-tail" ratios and reliance on individual (versus unit) replacement policies characteristic of a continuing orientation toward protracted conflict, the problem is nowhere more visible than in the U.S. Army. In contrast to the Soviet Army, for example, which fields a total of 173 divisions from a manpower base of 1.8 million active-duty personnel, the U.S. Army musters but 24 divisions (including eight National Guard divisions) from a base of 775,000 active-duty personnel. Finally, the present acute shortage in strategic lift capabilities—a shortage that cannot be overcome for at least a half decade—constrains U.S. ability to move military forces into the Gulf in a timely fashion.

Thus, existing U.S. forces, however re-equipped and strategically mobile, are simply insufficient in size to meet the requirements of defending the Gulf without reducing the capacity of the United States to meet its commitments elsewhere. In the absence either of larger forces, or of forces fundamentally restructured to maximize combat power, the price of effective deterrence in the Gulf is a degradation of deterrence in Europe and Northeast Asia. Conceivably, this dilemma could be resolved by Allied assumption of a greater portion of their own defense, thereby releasing U.S. forces for other missions. Unfortunately, prospects for compensatory Japanese and European investment in defense of the nec-

---

[42]John M. Collins and others, *Petroleum Imports from the Persian Gulf: Use of U.S. Armed Force to Ensure Supplies* (Washington, D.C.: Library of Congress Congressional Research Service, 1980), p. 16.

essary magnitude are not encouraging. Japan appears content to remain a military eunuch for the indefinite future; and many of America's NATO allies—including Germany—appear unwilling or unable to meet even pre-Afghanistan pledges for real increases in military spending devoted to the defense of Europe.[43]

Operational Unreadiness

The problems associated with reliance on forces already committed to non-Persian Gulf contingencies are compounded by a pervasive operational unreadiness that has characterized U.S. general purpose forces since Vietnam. Accelerating the pace at which U.S. ground, naval and tactical air forces can be moved to the Gulf is of little avail if those forces are not ready to move because they lack sufficient personnel, equipment, or training. Attributable largely to a decade of inadequate budgetary investment in Operations and Maintenance, and to the failure of the All-Volunteer Force to recruit and retain sufficient numbers of qualified people, the low readiness levels of U.S. conventional forces are incompatible with the demands of a sizable *unexpected* contingency in a distant area of the world where the United States does not enjoy secure military access ashore even in peacetime.

As shown in Table 4, using the Defense Department's own criteria for rating unit combat readiness (personnel, amount of equipment, quality of equipment, and training), less than 40 percent of U.S. general purpose forces may be regarded as fit to fight at the beginning of hostilities. The sole and notable exception is the Marine Corps, whose longstanding emphasis on being the "first to fight" is reflected in the fact that 70 percent of its units are rated as combat ready.

Lack of Reliable Client States

Another barrier to U.S. intervention in the Gulf is the lack of politically reliable and militarily competent U.S. client states in the region, whose assistance could be vital in a major contingency, particularly a prolonged one. The internal political fragility of potential friends and allies in the Gulf is exacerbated by the questionable capabilities and competence of their military establishments. The present Iraqi-Iranian war has done little

---

[43]Walter S. Mossberg, "Pentagon Warns Some Allies in Europe on Failing to Meet NATO Commitments," *Wall Street Journal,* October 3, 1980; and Leonard J. Downie, Jr., "U.S. Allies Cutting Defense Outlays Despite Vows to Bolster NATO," *Washington Post,* November 5, 1980.

to enhance the dismal military reputation of the Arab world, and national military forces on the Arabian peninsula are either negligible in size or questionable in quality, or both.[44] Enormous defense expenditures on the part of several Gulf states appear to have produced little in the way of technically competent, properly integrated, and well-led military forces. The large and experienced armies of Iraq, Iran, and Pakistan have been demoralized by defeat, revolution, or internal division along political or ethnic lines. In short, U.S. intervention forces could expect little effective support on the battlefield, even from host nations requesting intervention.

The adverse consequences of local military incompetence should not be underestimated, although U.S. intervention would, of course, benefit from it in contingencies involving aggression by a regional state. While many commentators pronounced the Guam (Nixon) Doctrine dead on arrival in the wake of the collapse of South Vietnam in 1975, the doctrine's fundamental premise remains as valid today as it was when promulgated in Guam in 1969: The sustained application of major U.S. military power in the Third World is not likely to succeed if unsupported by viable and competent local regimes capable of assuming a significant responsibility for the land battle. As noted, this is surely one of the principal geostrategic lessons of U.S. intervention in Indochina. Rushing to the defense of any nation either unwilling or sufficiently incapable of defending itself is to rush into the potential abyss of another Vietnam.[45]

As stressed in 1980 by then Under-Secretary of Defense Komer before the Senate Armed Services Committee,

The United States would be hard pressed to defend its interests in the [Indian Ocean and Persian Gulf] region if regional forces are not able or inclined to participate in their own defense. Accordingly, we would hope to have direct military support from regional states which are at risk.[46]

On what grounds, however, can the United States "hope to have direct military support from regional states which are at risk," particularly the kind of effective support required in the face of direct Soviet aggression or aggression by a Soviet client state? The availability of such support is

---

[44]For a comprehensive review of Gulf state military capabilities, see Mansur, "The Military Balance in the Persian Gulf . . ., *op. cit.*

[45]As then Secretary of Defense Brown noted in testimony before the Senate Armed Services Committee in 1980, "the United States cannot defend . . . people in the [Gulf] region who are not willing to participate in their own defense. You need a significant political base and . . . effort by the people in the region." *Hearings, op. cit.,* Part 1, p. 35.

[46]Prepared statement on the Indian Ocean and Rapid Deployment Force before the Senate Armed Services Committee, February 21, 1980, p. 3.

ultimately a function of the political stability of the regime supplying it; its effectiveness is a product of the size and competence of the regime's military forces. In the Persian Gulf, the West for decades enjoyed in the Shah of Iran a powerful and seemingly stable local client committed to the defense of shared interests. Yet, which potential Western client among the littoral states of the Persian Gulf and Indian Ocean today can be regarded as both politically stable and militarily competent? Somalia? Oman? Saudi Arabia? Kuwait? The United Arab Emirates? Pakistan? All of these states are governed by military regimes or semi-feudal monarchies whose social and political fragility renders them exceedingly vulnerable to internal overthrow by Soviet-sponsored leftist groups or the forces of religious fundamentalism now sweeping the House of Islam.

TABLE 4

Readiness of General Purpose Force Units by Service, 1980
(in percentages)

| | Readiness Category[1] | | | | |
| | Combat Ready | | Non-Combat Ready | | |
	C-1[2]	C-2[3]	C-3[4]	C-4[5]	C-5[6]
Army	—	37	25	38	—
Navy	3	28	33	15	21
Air Force	18	39	18	16	9
Marine Corps	—	70	30	—	—
Total	6	32	30	15	17

Source: Melvin R. Laird and Lawrence J. Korb, "The Precarious State of Our Armed Forces," Interservice, Fall 1980.

[1] Based on four criteria: personnel, amount of equipment, quality of equipment and training.
[2] Fully combat ready.
[3] Substantially combat ready (i.e., unit has only minor deficiencies).
[4] Marginally combat ready (i.e., unit has major deficiencies but can still perform its assigned missions).
[5] Not combat ready because of too many deficiencies.
[6] Not combat ready because unit is undergoing planned overhaul or maintenance.

The Burden of a Sagging Military Reputation

Overshadowing all of the above obstacles to successful U.S. military intervention in the Persian Gulf is the corrosive political effect of America's own declining military reputation. The question of whether the United

States is capable of competently employing military power is admittedly an unpleasant one.[47] The recurrent failure of American arms during the past thirty years, however, has undoubtedly raised this question in the Gulf and elsewhere, to the misfortune of the United States.

It should go without saying that military reputation, or the ability to use force successfully in defense of declared national interests, is desirable in a world where force remains the final arbiter of international disputes. Proven military prowess is indispensable to the United States, whose interests abroad are in fact being threatened and to whom others look for protection. Manifest incapacity to use force effectively tempts adversaries and discourages allies.

It is therefore important to recognize that the bungled attempt last April to free our hostages in Iran was but the latest page in a dismal chapter in American military history. Not since the Inchon landing has a significant U.S. military venture been crowned by success. On the contrary, our military performance since September 1950 suggests that we as a society may have lost touch with the art of war. Inchon was followed by the rout of American forces along the Yalu; Yalu by the Bay of Pigs fiasco; the Bay of Pigs by disaster in Indochina; Indochina by the fizzled raid to retrieve U.S. POWs thought to be confined in North Vietnam's Son Tay prison camp; Son Tay by the pyrrhic victory on Koh Tang Island in search of the crew of the hijacked *Mayaguez;* and *Mayaguez* by the debacle in the Iranian desert.[48]

The cumulative impact of this string of military miscarriages upon foreign perceptions of our military competence has been detrimental to U.S. fortunes abroad, particularly against the backdrop of a foreign policy that has made a virtue of irresolution when it comes to the employment of force even in defense of interests deemed vital.[49] It is hard to believe that

---

[47] See Jeffrey Record, "Is Our Military Incompetent?," *Newsweek,* December 22, 1980, and "The Fortunes of War," *Harpers,* April 1980; Edward N. Luttwak, "The American Style of Warfare and the Military Balance," *Survival,* March/April 1979, and "The Decline of American Military Leadership," *Parameters,* December 1980; Richard A. Gabriel and Paul L. Savage, *Crisis in Command, Mismanagement in the Army* (New York: Hill and Wang, 1978); Cincinnatus (pseudonym), *Self-Destruction: The Disintegration and Decay of the United States Army During the Vietnam Era* (New York: W. W. Norton, 1981); and Steven L. Canby, "General Purpose Forces," *International Security Review,* Fall 1980.

[48] The U.S. landings in Lebanon in 1958 and intervention in the Dominican Republic in 1965 were successful, although they can hardly be regarded as combat operations. The Lebanon landings were completely unopposed, and the Dominican intervention encountered negligible resistance.

[49] See Robert W. Tucker, "America in Decline: The Foreign Policy of 'Maturity'," *Foreign Affairs,* Fall 1980, pp. 449-484.

perception of a United States unwilling to use force and *unable to do so effectively* failed to influence the actions of Khomeini and the Kremlin during the past two years.

Although means of restoring America's declining military reputation are not at all apparent, its impact on U.S. fortunes in the Gulf has been profoundly deleterious, even among potential friends and allies. In the case of Saudi Arabia, the question of American military competence is but one of many issues that have damaged confidence in the United States.

It is one of the many ironies of the Carter Administration's foreign policy that while the U.S. is deeply enmeshed in planning measures to protect Saudi Arabia, and is almost obsessed with concern that Saudi Arabia may follow Iran, the Saudis now view the United States as the most serious threat to their own security, and Saudi Arabia's ability to provide the U.S. with a stable oil supply. This American "threat" to Saudi Arabia is the result of the seven major problems and trends in Saudi-U.S. relations:

The depth of Saudi Arabia's alignment with what the world perceives as a weak and ineffective U.S. Administration inevitably ties world perceptions of Saudi vulnerability to the growing feeling that the U.S. is not capable of effective and well planned action. The Saudis feel that almost inevitably, the image of U.S. weakness increases the willingness of other nations to test Saudi vulnerability.

The U.S. focus on military intervention capabilities in the Persian Gulf has been so awkwardly handled that many Saudis are becoming convinced that the U.S. is doing more to prepare to seize the Gulf oilfields in Saudi Arabia than to defend the Persian Gulf and Saudi Arabia.

Saudi reliance on U.S. military assistance creates such a serious risk that the Saudi military and much of Saudi society may become convinced that the Saudi regime is tied to an ally which will neither provide objective advice, nor the military equipment Saudi Arabia needs. These problems are reinforced by the lack of discipline shown by former and current members of the U.S. advisory team in publicizing their criticisms of both the Saudi government and the Saudi military effort.

The constant discussion of every indicator of internal instability in Saudi Arabia within the U.S. national security community now has the end result of publicizing every real or rumored problem in Saudi society throughout the Washington diplomatic community, and is acting to persuade more and more nations that the Saudis are both in trouble and vulnerable.

The continuing problem of the Camp David agreement: although the Saudi government has conspicuously opposed both the agreement and the lack of U.S. support for self-determination in Palestine since the agreement, it remains identified with the U.S.; thus, every further incident on the West Bank tends to increase the risk that opposition to the Saudi government will grow because of its continued ties to the United States.

U.S. pressure on Saudi Arabia to continue to produce oil at 9½ million barrels per day: a substantial portion of the royal family and most leading Saudi technocrats feel their government is wasting the national patrimony by producing more oil than Saudi Arabia conceivably needs to sell, and by underselling other exporting nations to keep world oil prices down. There is growing internal opposition to such sales, and in this case educated Saudis are joined by conservatives who see Saudi Arabia's high oil revenues as leading to uncontrollable change as Saudi society tries to cope with more income than it can effectively utilize.

Changes in U.S. law and tax structure have created a situation where the former partnership between the U.S. private sector and Saudi Arabia in major construction and development projects is being eroded to the point of destruction. While major increases in South Korean and other foreign corporate activity in Saudi Arabia were inevitable, U.S. policy is breaking the commercial links between the U.S. and Saudi Arabia that were of major aid in providing a secure source of assistance in development and economic growth.

These seven problems do not yet directly threaten Saudi stability or alignment with the United States. They are, however, steadily creating a climate which will virtually force the Saudi government to create a more visible distance between itself and the U.S. At best, they are probably forcing Saudi Arabia in the direction of a split with the U.S. over the military assistance effort, and another oil embargo in response to the Palestinian problem. At worst, a truly major crisis on the West Bank, or a badly handled U.S. military action in the Persian Gulf, could lead to a major internal political crisis and possibly trigger the overthrow of at least the pro-American portion of the Saudi government.

During the last four years, most Americans have become steadily more concerned with the image of U.S. weakness and indecisiveness that has increased with virtually every crisis in foreign affairs. Yet many Americans have not perceived the practical implications of the decline in U.S. power for our allies. The fall of the Shah, the failure of U.S. efforts to rescue the hostages, and American inability to do more than protest Soviet action in Afghanistan have had a powerful impact in the Middle East and Persian Gulf.

From a Saudi point of view, this image of American weakness has created the following problems:

Enough of the aftermath of Vietnam still lingers to cast into serious doubt U.S. willingness to intervene in any major conflict. This has been reinforced by American indecisiveness over the fall of the Shah and the Administration's near total silence on the once-dominant issue of hostages in Iran since the attempt to rescue them failed last April. For all the rhetoric about U.S. rapid deployment capabilities in the Persian Gulf, the real signal seems to be that the U.S. may not react to any threat to Saudi Arabia of any kind, and almost certainly will not react to anything less than the most overt attack.

This is compounded by a broad perception that the U.S. lacks the intelligence and special operations capabilities to deal with lesser threats. There is a broad perception in the Middle East and Persian Gulf area that the CIA and U.S. military intelligence is effectively hamstrung by the various legal and administrative constraints now placed on any U.S. covert action, and that the new generation of CIA employees lacks the background, training, and support to be effective.

President Carter is broadly perceived as well meaning, but weak and indecisive. There is the feeling that he will not act if even moderate care is exercised in any attempt to undermine the Saudi regime, or would temporize and vacillate if such action is slow and steady enough.

This already has led to a steady increase in the attempts of various liberation groups to undermine the governments of the other Gulf states. It has also led nations like Iraq and Kuwait to back as far away from the United States as they can in an attempt to avoid becoming targets for either Soviet or radical action against them. The result is that Saudi Arabia tends to become the key target for virtually every anti-U.S. interest in the Gulf. It is seen as a U.S. client state whose defense is dependent on an America which lacks the leadership to act.

If the U.S. seems preternaturally interested in every sign of Saudi instability, there is an almost equal Saudi interest in every indicator of growing American weakness, and that if the Carter Administration is spending much of its time watching the Saudi Royal Family the Saudi government is spending much of its time watching the Carter Administration.[50]

To sum up, obstacles to U.S. military intervention in the Persian Gulf abound. If intervention becomes necessary, to succeed it must overcome backbreaking distances and ferocious natural and battlefield environments. It also must be prepared to compensate for the absence of effective local assistance and of assured access to military facilities ashore in the region. Finally, intervention—at least for the next half-decade—must be carried out by forces not only thinly stretched by commitments outside the Gulf but also burdened by severe readiness problems and a declining military reputation.

---

[50]Mansur, "The American Threat to Saudi Arabia," *op. cit.*, pp. 47-50.

4. The Rapid Deployment Force

The present Rapid Deployment Force is an expression of three distinct sets of initiatives undertaken by the Carter Administration during the latter half of 1979 and the first half of 1980, although the conceptual origins of the RDF date back to 1977. The first set consists of strategic mobility initiatives aimed at increasing the speed with which U.S. forces can be deployed to the Persian Gulf or other logistically remote areas of the world. These initiatives include a planned expansion in the strategic airlift and sealift capabilities and a program to stockpile afloat in the Indian Ocean equipment for a full U.S. Marine division. The second set comprises organizational initiatives, notably the establishment of a new command headquarters—the Rapid Deployment Joint Task Force— charged with identifying, training, and planning the employment over- seas of rapidly deployable U.S. military units based in the United States. The third set of initiatives consists of diplomatic undertakings designed to attain contingent U.S. access to selected military facilities in the greater Gulf region, access that could prove critical to the success of any pro- longed U.S. intervention ashore in the region.

In reviewing these initiatives it is important to keep in mind the distinction between near-term and long-term capabilities—i.e., between forces already deployed or rapidly deployable to the Persian Gulf, and those expected to be so by the latter half of the 1980s. It is also important to distinguish between that portion of the Rapid Deployment Force that is to be stationed in the Gulf region itself, and "back-up" forces to be retained in the United States. The former, consisting largely of naval units and Marine Corps forces deployed afloat, would comprise the cutting edge of intervention in the Gulf; the latter, mostly U.S. Army and USAF tactical air units in the United States, constitutes a reinforcement pool.

Two fundamental assumptions appear to underlie the RDF initiatives to date. The first is that the key to successful U.S. military intervention in the Persian Gulf lies not in larger or restructured forces but rather in getting existing U.S. forces there faster. This assumption is evident in a host of official pronouncements. In his *Annual Report* for fiscal year 1981, then Secretary of Defense Harold Brown stated that the problem was not the lack of enough forces but rather the inability to "move them in force and with great rapidity to an area of crisis."[51]

---

[51]*Department of Defense Annual Report, Fiscal Year 1981* (Washington, D.C.: Department of Defense, 1980), p. 9.

In subsequent testimony before the Senate Armed Services Committee, Brown reiterated his conviction that the "rapid deployment forces exist. What is needed is additional lift capability and some reorganization. . . ."[52] Brown's definition of the problem was echoed by then Under-Secretary of Defense Robert Komer and Lieutenant General Paul X. Kelley, the newly appointed commander of the Rapid Deployment Joint Task Force. According to Komer,

Rapid deployment forces are not new. We have had them for several decades. They consist of existing forces of all services which have been designated to be ready to deploy on short notice. However, the nature of the threats in the 1980s, especially in the Persian Gulf area, demands that we be able to do it better and do it faster.[53]

And Kelley warned that

all of the combat power of the United States is absolutely worthless if it is just sitting here in the United States. We have to come to grips with something that we have neglected for a number of years, and that is strategic mobility.[54]

This almost exclusive emphasis on strategic mobility was underscored by Under-Secretary Komer's earlier testimony that "We are not contemplating any major force structure changes for the Rapid Deployment Force."[55]

The second assumption governing the RDF is that the actual deployment of RDF forces ashore in the Persian Gulf region during a crisis is not likely to be contested. The presumption of administrative (i.e., unopposed) entry is manifest in the character of the proposed new CX strategic transport aircraft and maritime prepositioning ship, both of which are unarmed. It is further evident in the absence of requests for any increase in the present—and woefully inadequate levels—of amphibious shipping and other forcible-entry capabilities.

Indeed, the primary planning emphasis within the RDJTF seems to be on avoiding contested entry by means of a preemptive strategy that, according to General Kelley, allows the United States to "get forces into an area rapidly, irrespective of size. . . ."[56]

---

[52]*Hearings, op. cit.*, Part 1, p. 62.

[53]*Ibid.*, Part 1, p. 496.

[54]*Ibid.*, Part 5, p. 3175.

[55]*Ibid.*, Part 3, p. 1257.

[56]News Briefing by Kelley, at the Pentagon, June 18, 1980. See also Richard Halloran, "Gaps in Training and Equipment Hinder Rapid Deployment Force," *New York Times,* September 26, 1980; John K. Cooley, "US Rapid Strike Force: How to Get There First with the Most," *Christian Science Monitor,* April 11, 1980; and Bernard Weinraub, "Warning Crucial to Air and Sea Transport Abilities," *New York Times,* September 26, 1980.

In then Secretary of Defense Harold Brown's view,

What is important is the ability to move forces into the region with the numbers, mobility, and firepower to *preclude initial adversary forces from reaching vital targets.* It is not necessary for our initial units to be able to defeat the whole force an adversary might eventually have in place. It is also not necessary for us to await the firing of the first shot or the prior arrival of hostile forces; many of our forces can be moved upon strategic warning, and some upon receipt of even very early and ambiguous indicators.[57]

As noted, the viability of such a preemptive strategy, especially in an area of the world where the Soviet Union enjoys the advantage of geographical proximity, hinges entirely upon a robust intelligence community capable of providing "strategic warning" and a political willingness to act boldly "upon receipt of even very early and ambiguous indicators."

Before turning to an exploration of the RDF as it now stands, which is the purpose of this chapter, it is worthwhile to recall that neither the concept of rapid deployment nor the existence of rapidly deployable forces is new. In its naval, Marine, and airborne forces the United States has always possessed rapidly deployable military power. The need for a special, global strike force that could be quickly deployed to areas of the world where U.S. forces are not already established ashore (as in Europe and Korea) was perceived in the early 1960s by the Kennedy Administration. In 1962 the U.S. Strike Command was created, consisting mainly of designated U.S. Army units located in the United States whose rapid deployability to overseas trouble spots was to be ensured by the development and procurement of a new strategic transport aircraft, the C-5A, and a new sealift vessel, the Fast Deployment Logistics (FDL) ship. The rationale underlying the U.S. Strike Command was provided by Secretary of Defense Robert S. McNamara in testimony before the Senate:

Either we can station numbers of men and quantities of equipment and supplies overseas near all potential trouble spots, or we can maintain a much smaller force in a central reserve in the United States and deploy it rapidly where needed.[58]

In McNamara's judgment, the greater cost of the former alternative argued strongly for "a mobile 'fire brigade' reserve, centrally located . . . and ready for quick deployment to any threatened area in the world. . . ."[59]

---

[57]Secretary of Defense Harold Brown, Remarks to the Council of Foreign Relations, New York, March 6, 1980. (Emphasis added.)

[58]Quoted in Michael T. Klare, "Have R.D.F., Will Travel," *The Nation,* March 8, 1980, p. 257.

[59]*Ibid.,* p. 257.

Although Congress funded the C-5A, which together with the C-141 remains the backbone of the U.S. Military Airlift Command, the proposed logistics ship was defeated. Widening American involvement in Vietnam not only diverted military resources away from the Strike Command and other missions but also led to rising concern within the Congress that the very existence of a new intervention force would invite another Vietnam. As the late Senator Richard B. Russell, then Chairman of the Senate Armed Services Committee, pointedly remarked, "If it is easy for us to go anywhere and do anything, then we will always be going somewhere and doing something."[60]

At the beginning of 1972, as part of a major effort to streamline the U.S. military command structure, the Strike Command was replaced by the U.S. Readiness Command (REDCOM). Like its predecessor, REDCOM has no specific regional responsibility; it consists of U.S.-based forces slated to reinforce other unified commands overseas, especially in Europe and Korea. In the immediate post-Vietnam era, the prospect of U.S. military intervention outside Europe and Northeast Asia was regarded as highly unlikely. Also in 1972, the jurisdiction of the U.S. European Command (EUCOM) was extended to include the Red Sea, Persian Gulf, and Iran; three years later, the U.S. Pacific Command was granted responsibility for the entire Indian Ocean to the east coast of Africa.

The origins of the present Rapid Deployment Force may be traced to Presidential Directive (PD) 18, which was issued in August 1977, shortly after the Carter Administration took office. The product of a comprehensive review of U.S. security commitments and capabilities, PD-18 called for the creation of a "quick-reaction" force composed largely of light infantry formations backed up by expanded strategic airlift and sealift.

Little in the way of supporting budgetary initiatives was visible, however, until early 1980, following the seizure of U.S. diplomatic personnel in Tehran in November 1979 and the Soviet invasion of Afghanistan six weeks later. Although press reports made frequent reference to plans for a "Quick Strike Force" and "Unilateral Intervention Corps," the pre-Afghanistan defense budgets of the Carter Administration (fiscal years 1978, 1979, and 1980) reflected a continuing preoccupation with U.S. Army, tactical air, and other NATO-oriented forces at the expense of surface naval, U.S. Marine Corps, and other forces associated with intervention in areas where U.S. forces are not prepositioned ashore. This preoccupation vanished in the fiscal 1981 budget.

---

[60]*Ibid.*, p. 258.

Strategic Mobility Initiatives

RDF-related strategic mobility initiatives are designed to increase the speed with which U.S. ground forces in the United States could be moved to the Persian Gulf. Their aim, according to former Secretary of Defense Harold Brown, is "to allow us to deploy very substantial forces to [the Gulf] in about one-third the time that it takes now."[61]

Moving sizable ground forces from one continent to another under crisis conditions (when time is the great adversary) has always been a difficult and costly task. Naval and air forces possess inherent intercontinental (strategic) mobility. Ground forces do not, since they can neither fly nor swim. The United States, separated by vast expanses of ocean from its principal defense commitments, has relied upon two means of endowing its U.S.-based ground forces with strategic mobility. The first has entailed the creation and maintenance of fleets of cargo ships and long-range transport aircraft capable of "lifting" both the equipment and personnel of ground forces overseas. The second means has been the pre-positioning of equipment in areas of anticipated combat, thus requiring, in a crisis, the movement only of personnel.

Increases in prepositioning of equipment and "lift" capabilities are prominent features of the present Rapid Deployment Force. Indeed, the most distinctive of all RDF-related strategic mobility initiatives is the plan to preposition equipment at sea.

Maritime Prepositioning. Present Department of Defense plans call for the prepositioning, by fiscal year 1987, of a full Marine Corps division's worth of equipment and 30-day supply of ammunition, fuel, and spare parts aboard twelve specially-designed logistics ships, known as Maritime Prepositioning Ships (MPS). The ships, the first four of which are scheduled for delivery by fiscal 1983 (to be followed by four more in fiscal 1985, and the final four by fiscal 1987), are to be stationed in the Indian Ocean, utilizing Diego Garcia as their principal anchorage. Essentially unarmed floating warehouses to be manned by civilian crews, the MPS will be capable of unloading their cargoes "over the beach" by means of lighters carried aboard, although only in a benign (i.e., non-hostile) environment.

Concern over the unavailability until 1982 of the first MPS propelled the Department of Defense to authorize the creation of an interim force known as the Near-Term Prepositioned Ship (NTPS) force, which was deployed to the Indian Ocean in July 1980. The NTPS force consists of seven

---

[61]*Hearings, op. cit.,* Part 1, p. 25.

existing ships[62] containing "equipment, supplies, fuel and water sufficient to support a Marine amphibious brigade of about 12,000 men, and to sustain several USAF fighter squadrons."[63] The amount of the brigade's equipment already afloat in the Indian Ocean is impressive (see Table 5), and would permit the United States, within a matter of days, to bring to bear ashore in the Persian Gulf a sizable ground force.[64] In the absence of prepositioning (i.e., the retention of the brigade's equipment in the United States), it would take several weeks to deploy the brigade to the Persian Gulf.

The decision to rely on maritime—as opposed to ashore—prepositioning was dictated by the refusal of even friendly Gulf states to permit the stationing of U.S. forces or war materiel on their own territory. Even in a politically permissible environment, however, maritime prepositioning would still be preferable.

We are proposing to preposition on ships instead of prepositioning ashore, as we do in Europe. In Europe, of course, we know from where the enemy is coming. The terrain has been studied and fought over for centuries. The axes of advance are well known. So, we can preposition the stuff on land. But when you look at the enormous distances in the Indian Ocean, where you might have a contingency in the Red Sea or the Persian Gulf or in the Indian Ocean, maritime prepositioning is militarily advantageous and it solves the political problem by not putting it on land.

If we were to stockpile, let us say . . . two division sets of equipment in Somalia and the crisis turned out to be in Iran or we went to the defense of Saudi Arabia or Kuwait, we would then have to send out ships and airplanes, pick up the equipment in Somalia and move it 2,000 miles farther to the Persian Gulf. Under the circumstances it would be much more flexible for us to have the equipment on ships, and in an emergency, start those ships moving toward the area where we thought the contingency would arise.[65]

----

[62]Three commercial roll-on-roll-off vessels capable of handling armored vehicles, artillery, and other large items of rolling stock; two standard break-bulk ships; and two tankers, one for fuel and the other for water. Unlike the MPS, none of the seven ships of the interim force is capable of "over the beach" operations; all require port facilities to unload their cargo.

[63]Testimony of Deputy Secretary of Defense W. Graham Claytor, Jr., in Hearings, op. cit., Part 2, p. 1132.

[64]According to the Department of Defense, "the only significant items of equipment which will not be prepositioned are individual and crew-served weapons and equipment such as packs, helmets, rifles, machine-guns . . . and other specific items which do not lend themselves to long term storage such as aircraft and highly technical electronics equipment which, if stored, would be difficult to maintain in or rapidly bring to an operational readiness status. These items would be [flown] in along with the troops." Hearings, ibid., Part 1, p. 490.

[65]Testimony of Under-Secretary of Defense Robert Komer, in Hearings, ibid., Part 3, pp. 1248-1249.

TABLE 5

Major Items of Equipment for a Marine Amphibious Brigade Prepositioned Afloat in the Indian Ocean, 1980

Type of Equipment	Quantity
Tracked vehicles:	
Tanks (M-60)	53
Armored amphibians (LVTP-7)	95
Tank retrievers	5
155mm howitzer (SP)	12
Bulldozers	9
Total	174
Wheeled vehicles:	
5-ton trucks	135
2½-ton trucks	177
¼-ton trucks	270
Total	582
Other major items:	
Hawk launchers	6
105mm howitzer (towed)	18
155mm howitzer (towed)	6
Redeye launchers	90
Trailers, vans, generators, etc.	1,519
Total	1,639
Total items	2,395

Source: Department of Defense Authorization for Appropriations for Fiscal Year 1981, Hearings before the Committee on Armed Services, United States Senate, 96th Congress, 2nd Session, 1980, Part 5, p. 3159.

Enhanced Strategic Airlift. With the exception of a single Marine division, both ground and tactical air forces assigned to the RDF will be withheld in the United States along with their equipment. To enhance the strategic mobility of the nonprepositioned portion of the RDF the Department of Defense has sought to increase present levels of airlift and sealift capabilities. With respect to strategic airlift, current plans call for development and production of a new strategic transport, known as the CX;

extension of the service life of the existing C-5A; an increase in the cargo capacity of the existing C-141; procurement of additional KC-10 tanker aircraft; and modification of commercial aircraft for the military transport role.

It is widely conceded that present U.S. strategic airlift capabilities, centered in the U.S. Military Airlift Command's 77 C-5A and 276 C-141 aircraft, are insufficient to meet the demands of a NATO contingency alone, to say nothing of a simultaneous contingency in the Persian Gulf.[66] The Congressional Budget Office has estimated that it would "take as long as five weeks to deliver a light and a heavy division to the Persian Gulf region by airlift alone, assuming that *all* airlift resources were available for the deployment."[67]

In its fiscal 1981 budget submission, the Carter Administration accordingly requested funds to initiate development of a new strategic transport aircraft. From the beginning, however, the CX encountered problems in the Congress. Considering the program's high cost—estimated at between $6.6 and $12 billion for a total of 130-200 aircraft (depending on its size), the unsatisfactory design of the plane,[68] its unavailability in substantial numbers until the late 1980s, and the comparative attractiveness of maritime prepositioning as a means of enhancing strategic mobility, the Congress slashed the request and directed the Department of Defense to reappraise U.S. airlift requirements for the Persian Gulf.[69]

Congressional support was forthcoming, however, for other airlift enhancement programs, all of which were initiated long before the Soviet invasion of Afghanistan, although they were subsequently publicized by the Carter Administration as Rapid Deployment Force initiatives. The

---

[66]The gap between lift capabilities and requirements for NATO led the Carter Administration to preposition in Europe extra sets of equipment for three U.S. divisions based in the United States, bringing the total to five such divisions (together with five division equivalents deployed in Europe).

[67]*U.S. Airlift Forces: Enhancement Alternatives for NATO and Non-NATO Contingencies* (Washington, D.C.: Congressional Budget Office, 1979), p. 56. (Emphasis added.)

[68]The design represented an attempt to combine the lift capacity of a large transport and the short take-off and landing capabilities of the defunct and much smaller tactical transport, the Advanced Medium STOL (AMST). The proposed CX design, both smaller and possessing less range than the existing C-5A, and capable of carrying only one main battle tank, led some critics to conclude that a reopening of the C-5A production line would be more cost-effective than development of a new aircraft.

[69]*Conference Report of the House and Senate Committees on Armed Services on Department of Defense Authorization Act, 1981,* Report No. 96-895, 96th Congress, 2nd Session, 1980. See also "Rebuff to CX," *Aviation Week and Space Technology,* April 7, 1980; and Benjamin F. Schemmer, "USAF Asked Why Not an Updated C-5A Instead of New CX, Reaffirms CX Need," *Armed Forces Journal,* April 1980.

programs include: (1) modifying the wings of the C-5A to increase its service life to 30,000 hours; (2) lengthening the fuselage of the C-141 to increase its cargo capacity by as much as 30 percent; (3) modifying commercial "jumbo" jets for potential military transport operations; and (4) procurement of 26 KC-10 tanker aircraft to supplement the present aging fleet of KC-135s.

Unfortunately, these programs, even if pursued to completion, would have only a marginal impact on the rate at which the United States could "close" ground forces to the Persian Gulf by air. In the judgment of the Congressional Budget Office,

major procurement of new . . . planes would be required to reduce delivery time substantially . . . . it would take a very large procurement of new aircraft—as many as . . . 100 new C-5s—to reduce closure times by a week for one division or two weeks for a two-division force.[70]

Yet "a very large procurement of new aircraft" would entail enormous opportunity costs. As noted by then Under-Secretary Komer, "the most cost-effective way to provide heavy equipment rapidly in the Indian Ocean is to preposition it on ships that are out there,"[71] which leads to the query raised by Senator Gary Hart during the debate over the CX: "The fundamental question is: Why are we going to build the CX? We have adequate airlift to move people. If the best way to move equipment is by sea, why spend $6 billion to build this airplane?"[72]

Indeed, the most compelling argument against the CX remains the greater cost-effectiveness of maritime prepositioning. In contrast to the $6-12 billion procurement price tag for a fleet of new strategic air transports, each capable of lifting but one main battle tank, the entire cost of pre-positioning the equipment of a full Marine division aboard twelve new Maritime Prepositioning Ships amounts to $4.076 billion.[73] The charter and operating costs of the seven-ship Near-Term Prepositioned Ship force, containing the equipment of a Marine brigade, total $790.8 million for the period 1980-1986.[74]

---

[70]U.S. Airlift Forces . . ., op. cit., p. 56.

[71]Hearings, op. cit., Part 1, p. 457.

[72]Ibid., Part 1, p. 463. An excellent and detailed analysis of the cost-ineffectiveness of airlift versus sealift for the rapid deployment mission is contained in Dov S. Zakheim, "Airlifting the Marine Corps: Mismatch or Wave of the Future?," a paper prepared for the Conference on Projection of Power: Perspectives, Perceptions, and Logistics, Boston, The Fletcher School of Law and Diplomacy, Tufts University, April 23-25, 1980.

[73]Ibid., Part 6, p. 3285. This figure includes the purchase price of all twelve MPS ships and associated operations and maintenance costs for the period 1980-1987.

[74]Ibid, Part 6, p. 3286.

Enhanced Sealift. The principal means of moving U.S.-based RDF ground forces to the Persian Gulf is by sea. To enhance the rapidity of deployment, the Department of Defense plans to purchase eight 33-knot Sealand SL-7 container ships and one Seabee barge carrier. The ships, which will cost a total of $341.5 million,[75] are commercially-owned but no longer commercially competitive. Capable of moving a U.S. Army mechanized division to the Persian Gulf in 15-19 days,[76] the SL-7 ships would be stationed at "load-out" ports in the United States, ready at a moment's notice to begin loading up the equipment of RDF-earmarked units.

To sum up, the strategic mobility initiatives associated with the Rapid Deployment Force are aimed at both increasing U.S. military power inside the Persian Gulf region (through the vehicle of maritime prepositioning) and increasing the pace at which U.S. military power outside the region can be deployed to it (through expanded airlift and sealift capabilities). Forces prepositioned in the region, supplemented by deployed naval units, would form the cutting edge of any U.S. military intervention in the Gulf; they would be reinforced by nonprepositioned forces withheld in the United States.

The Rapid Deployment Joint Task Force

The Rapid Deployment Joint Task Force was formally established on March 1, 1980 under the command of U.S. Marine Lieutenant General Paul X. Kelley. The purpose of the RDJTF, in General Kelley's words, is

> to plan the employment of designated forces, to jointly train and exercise them, and to ultimately deploy and employ them in response to contingencies threatening U.S. interests anywhere in the world. In essence, to provide the essential command and control that will bring together, in a synergistic way, the capabilities of our four services.[77]

Formations designated by the RDJTF to date for the rapid deployment mission include several USAF tactical fighter squadrons, four U.S. Army divisions, selected Marine Corps units, and assorted combat and combat service support elements. The Army divisions, which are the 82nd Airborne, 101st Airborne (Air Assault), the 9th Infantry, and the 24th (Mechanized) Infantry divisions, have two things in common: all are based in the United States, and all are simultaneously earmarked for NATO con-

---

[75]*Ibid.*, Part 6, p. 3286. Potential modifications to the SL-7 vessels vary in cost from $10-$80 million per ship.

[76]*Ibid.*, Part 2, p. 1140.

[77]*Hearings, op. cit.*, Part 1, p. 441.

tingencies.[78] The same is true of RDF-slated tactical air units and some Marine Corps forces that would be utilized in a Persian Gulf contingency.[79]

More significant, as shown in Table 6, is the fact that with the exception of the Army's 24th (Mechanized) Infantry Division and 194th Armored Brigade, all ground combat units designated by the RDJTF for rapid deployment are light, foot-mobile infantry units possessing little organic tactical mobility or firepower.[80] Despite the questionable suitability of such units for likely combat environments in the Gulf region (see discussion in Chapter 3), no significant changes in their equipment, force structure, or tactical doctrine are being contemplated (the 9th Infantry Division is the sole exception).

The total manpower associated with RDF-designated units approaches 200,000, together with approximately 100,000 reservists whose call-up would be necessary to support them.[81] The size and composition of rapid deployment forces actually committed to a Persian Gulf contingency, however, would be governed by the contingency's specific requirements. As explained by RDJTF Commander Lt. General Kelley,

Our task is to provide a capability for deploying force packages, of varying size and structure, to any region of the world. This is neither a separate nor discrete category of forces of fixed size; i.e., 50,000 or 100,000 man force. Rather the concept calls for a central "reservoir," composed primarily of CONUS-based units from which forces can be drawn to cope with a specific contingency. Obviously, the size and composition of the force selected will depend on what is determined to be our mission. Forces could be developed capable of responding to situations ranging from minimum application of force to mid-intensity combat. One could draw a building block analogy. . . .[82]

---

[78]Testimony of Army Chief of Staff, Edward C. Meyer, in *ibid.*, Part 2, p. 684. The 82nd is based at Ft. Bragg, North Carolina; the 101st at Ft. Campbell, Kentucky; and the 24th at Ft. Stewart, Georgia.

[79]Specific Marine Corps formations have not been designated for the RDF. "The Marine Corps commitment to the RDJTF will be scenario dependent. As plans are developed, we envisage Marine commitment which could range from a show of force or on-scene presence of a Marine Amphibious Unit (MAU) of approximately 1,800 Marines up to a commitment of one or more Marine Amphibious Forces (MAFs). A MAF is comprised of approximately 49,000 Marines." Testimony of Marine Corps Commandant Robert H. Barrow in *ibid.*, Part 2, p. 856.

[80]Although the 101st Airborne (Air Assault) Division and 6th Cavalry (Air Combat) Brigade rely upon helicopters for tactical mobility, helicopters are more weather-constrained and prone to maintenance failure than wheeled or tracked armored fighting vehicles.

[81]Interview with General Volney Warner, Commander, U.S. Readiness Command in "The RDF: What's Been Done, What Should Have Been Done," *Defense Week,* June 30, 1980.

[82]Prepared statement on the Indian Ocean and Rapid Deployment Forces before the Senate Armed Services Committee, February 21, 1980, pp. 2-3.

TABLE 6

Tentative Rapid Deployment
Joint Task Force Composition, 1980.

Unit	NATO Earmarked?	Light (L)/ Heavy (H)
Ground Forces		
(Army)		
18th Airborne Corps HQ	No	L
82nd Airborne Division	Yes	L
101st Air Assault Division	Yes	L
9th Infantry Division	Yes	L
24th Mechanized Division	Yes	H
194th Armored Brigade	No	H
6th Cavalry (Air Combat) Brigade	Yes	L
2 Ranger Infantry Battalions	Yes	L
(Marine Corps)		
1 Marine Amphibious Force	?	L
U.S. Air Force Units		
1 Air Force Hq	?	
12 tactical fighter squadrons	Yes	
2 tactical reconnaissance squadrons	Yes	
2 tactical airlift wings	No	
U.S. Navy Forces		
3 carrier battle groups	Some[1]	
1 surface action group	Some	
5 aerial patrol squadrons	Some	

Source: Information provided to the author by sources in the Department of Defense.

[1]A significant proportion of U.S. naval vessels currently deployed in the Indian Ocean belong to the U.S. 6th Fleet in the Mediterranean. Maintenance of a naval presence in the Indian Ocean at the expense of NATO-oriented naval forces is likely to continue throughout the decade.

Unfortunately, despite this rhetorical allegiance to the sound concept of "task-organizing" (i.e., tailoring the size and structure of a military response to the specific character of the threat), the paramount focus among force planners at MacDill Air Force Base, and especially within the U.S. Army's Readiness Command, seems to be that of simply getting more U.S. forces of any kind to the Persian Gulf in the shortest amount of time. In an interview with the *Washington Post* published in October 1980, Army Lt. General Volney F. Warner, head of the U.S. Readiness Command, virtually defined the success or failure of future U.S. military intervention in terms of the rate at which U.S. troops in the United States could be deployed to the Persian Gulf.[83] Noting that it would currently take the United States some 21 days to lift the 82nd Airborne Division and a single Marine brigade (a total force of 35,000 men) to the Gulf,[84] Warner stated that although such a force would not be able to deal successfully with a serious Soviet threat, it would "not [be] too big a force to lose." According to Warner, prospects for successful intervention would not emerge until 1985, when the realization of planned strategic mobility enhancement programs presumably will enable the United States within 21 days to generate a force equivalent to the 80,000-man Soviet force in Afghanistan.

On paper, all RDF units deployed to the Persian Gulf would be placed under the operational command of Lieutenant General P. X. Kelley, the designated commander of the RDJTF. Yet General Kelley has no authority to determine which forces would be assigned to him, most of which are "owned" by the Army-controlled U.S. Readiness Command (REDCOM). Moreover, as of this writing, the Army has succeeded in transferring much of the planning functions for Persian Gulf contingencies from the RDJTF to REDCOM; the result has been to deprive the commander of the RDF of the necessary authority to determine in advance how he would employ forces to be placed under his command.

Indeed, the present organization and composition of the Rapid Deployment Force are largely the product of intense interservice rivalry, especially between the U.S. Army and Marine Corps, for bureaucratic domination of the most significant U.S. military mission of the 1980s. The Army, whose current size and force structure is justified almost exclusively by the U.S. commitment to the conventional defense of Central Europe, is understandably concerned over the prospect of a future reduction in or

---

[83] George C. Wilson, "Outlook Grim in a War for Mideast Oil," *Washington Post,* October 28, 1980.

[84] This would seem to be a highly optimistic estimate. In the fall of 1980, an RDF exercise entailing the movement by air to Egypt of a single, 900-man U.S. Army infantry battalion took six days to complete.

even termination of that commitment, as the result either of greater Allied self-defense efforts or of a "Finlandized" Western Europe.[85] Accordingly, the Army views "ownership" of the rapid deployment mission as critical to its future role and status within the U.S. defense establishment.

The Marine Corps regards the rapid deployment mission as equally vital to its own future. The size and continuing orientation of the Corps toward amphibious assault has been increasingly difficult to justify since the Inchon landing, particularly against a backdrop of declining levels of amphibious shipping and naval gunfire support capabilities.[86] Moreover, the Corps, which has always regarded itself as the Nation's rapid deployment force, possesses a level of strategic mobility and other unique capabilities that lend themselves to the mission.

As originally conceived, the RDF was to be virtually an all-U.S. Army force, consisting of a pool of U.S.-based units containing 100,000-110,000 men and under the control of the U.S. Readiness Command, which has always been headed by an Army officer. The force's strategic mobility was to be provided by the present lift capabilities of the U.S. Military Airlift Command and the 50-odd ships of the U.S. Military Sealift Command. The inherent deficiencies of such a force soon became apparent. The comparative strategic immobility of the Army's heavy NATO-oriented formations; the unsatisfactory readiness levels of light RDF-slated Army units in the United States; the shortfalls in strategic lift; the exclusion of the Marine Corps' unique capabilities; and the unsuitability of the ponderous U.S. Readiness Command for intervention operations in the Persian Gulf—quickly convinced many that, in the words of one noted critic, "the highly touted fast-deployment force . . . should be more appropriately called the last deployment force."[87]

Accordingly, by the spring of 1980 significant changes in the organizational character of the RDF had been made. Prominent among them was a decision to create a separate and independent command for the RDF—the Rapid Deployment Joint Task Force (RDJTF)—to be headed, on a rotating basis, by either a Marine or an Army general. Under strong pressure from the Army, however, which saw in an independent, Corps-led RDJTF the loss of control over the rapid deployment mission, the

---

[85]These concerns have been repeatedly expressed to the author in conversations with the Chief of Staff and with other high-ranking Army officers.

[86]See, for example, Martin Binkin and Jeffrey Record, *Where Does the Marine Corps Go From Here?* (Washington, D.C.: Brookings Institution, 1976).

[87]Senator Sam Nunn, quoted in "U.S. Said to Lag on a Mobile Force for Use in 'Brush-Fire' Situations," *op. cit.*, p. 1.

Department of Defense subsequently placed the RDJTF under REDCOM. In so doing, it granted the Army ultimate authority over forces earmarked for rapid deployment by the commander of the RDJTF.

The result is a command structure oriented more toward interservice combat than preparation for combat against a foreign enemy.[88] Bitterness between the Army and Marine Corps at Florida's MacDill Air Force Base, where both REDCOM and the RDJTF are headquartered, is particularly profound.[89]

The command mess at MacDill Air Force Base is but part of the problem. Lines of operational authority are equally tangled in the greater Gulf region itself. No unified U.S. command exists in the region. On the contrary, responsibility for the Persian Gulf and adjacent land masses is assigned to the U.S. European Command, whereas the Indian Ocean remains the responsibility of the U.S. Pacific Command. The line of jurisdiction separating the two commands runs right through the critical Strait of Hormuz.

The potentially disastrous consequences of the present command arrangements have drawn the attention of a growing number of critics, including former Secretary of Defense James R. Schlesinger:

A new command can at least point out serious deficiencies, so surely that is a sign of progress. Yet one can never be sure. One must recall that the [Carter] Administration's response earlier to the discovery of a Soviet combat brigade in Cuba was—to establish a new headquarters at Key West. Similarly, the chief military concomitant to the very ambitious mission embodied in the Carter Doctrine was the establishment of a new headquarters for the RDF—along with some frenetic planning and some slight action.

One can scarcely overemphasize the importance of command/control in assessing the chances for success. Particularly is this the case when adjustments of service roles and missions are in prospect. One need only recall the recent abortive rescue mission in the Iranian desert to understand both the significance and the delicacy of command/control arrangements. Let us therefore review what has happened with the RDF.

A Marine general has been placed in charge of the RDF. The Army, fearing that it might be foreclosed in large degree from the most significant new mission of the decade, appealed to Higher Authority regarding the initial command arrangements. Consequently, the RDF has now been made subordinate to Readiness

---

[88]Robert C. Toth, "Military's Bureaucracy Curbs Emergency Unit," *Los Angeles Times,* December 1, 1980.

[89]Richard Burt, "Army and Marines in Battle Over Command of Rapid Deployment Force," *New York Times,* December 10, 1980.

Command—by the sheerest coincidence commanded by an Army general. In the event that the balloon goes up, that would provide the Army with suitable terrain from which to commence bureaucratic combat. In the event of trouble, the Marine general would become commander-in-chief of Indian Ocean forces. Yet he has no lines of authority over the forces that he hopes would be assigned to him, if he were told to go. He can start planning now to negotiate for the forces (if they are at all ready) with which presumably he would fight.[90]

Gaining Access to Regional Military Facilities

The refusal of states in the Gulf region to permit the permanent stationing in peacetime of U.S. combat forces on their territory has compelled the Department of Defense to rely on a combination of maritime prepositioning and diplomatic arrangements that would grant the United States contingent access to selected military facilities in the region. Such access could be logistically critical to the success of any prolonged U.S. military intervention ashore. Diego Garcia, the sole U.S.-controlled military base in the region, is also to be upgraded, although its size and location make it unsuitable as a base for staging major military operations in the Gulf.[91]

As of this writing, agreements have been concluded with Kenya, Somalia, and Oman for contingent U.S. access to the facilities listed in Table 7 and shown in Map 3. Although the agreements have not been published, they appear to entail the following provisions:[92]

- United States to enjoy standard access and status of forces arrangements.

- No U.S. security commitments to host country or formal obligation to sell weapons, although security assistance is implied.[93]

- United States to be granted discretionary use rights with respect to facilities in question, although United States must "consult" with host government on major exercises and deployments.

---

[90]James R. Schlesinger, "Rapid (?) Deployment (?) Force (?)," *Washington Post,* September 24, 1980.

[91]Planned expansion of the U.S. base at Diego Garcia, scheduled to be completed in 1982, encompasses the construction of (1) a modern communications station, (2) a 12,000-foot runway, (3) a deep-water anchorage, (4) fuel storage facilities, (5) a fuel loading and unloading pier for fleet oilers, (6) an aircraft maintenance hangar, (7) additional warehouses, and (8) personnel support buildings. See *Hearings, op. cit.,* Part 1, p. 318.

[92]Based on information provided to the author by sources in the Department of Defense.

[93]See, for example, Michael Getler, "U.S. Would Link Aid to Access to Bases," *Washington Post,* February 28, 1980; and Lars-Erik Nelson, "Oman Asks Some Return for U.S. Aid," *New York Times,* October 16, 1980.

MAP 3
U.S. "Access" Facilities in the Persian Gulf/Indian Ocean Region

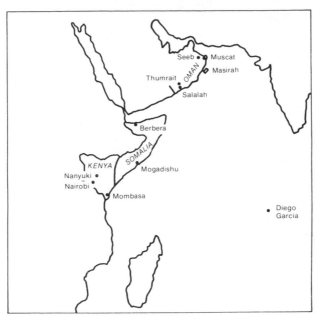

TABLE 7
Persian Gulf Region Facilities to Which U.S. Military Forces Have Been Granted Limited/Contingent Access, 1980.

Country	Facility	Type
OMAN	Seeb	airfield/port
	Thumrait	airfield
	Muscat	airfield/port
	Salalah	airfield
	Masirah	airfield
SOMALIA	Berbera	airfield/port
	Mogadishu	airfield/port
KENYA	Mombasa	port
	Nairobi	airfield
	Nanyuki	airfield

Source: Information provided to the author by sources in the Department of Defense.

- Host government to retain sovereign rights over all facilities and ownership of all real property.

- United States to pay for services rendered by host government, plus proportionate share of facility maintenance.

- United States to be allowed to upgrade facilities at its own expense.[94]

- Agreements to remain in force for ten years.

While the arrangements concluded to date with Oman, Kenya, and Somalia, and other countries in the area are certainly no substitute for U.S.-controlled bases in the region, they are not without benefits. Egypt, for example, has permitted the United States to exercise its military forces—including elements of the RDF—on Egyptian soil;[95] Oman has received overnight visits from U.S. carrier-based aircraft; and Saudi Arabia requested and received deployment of U.S. AWACS surveillance aircraft during the Iraqi-Iranian war.

On the other hand, there is little ground for confidence that, "given a serious contingency [in the Gulf] . . . we would be granted the necessary access as well as the necessary overflight and refueling privileges."[96] As noted in the preceding chapter, the same internal political considerations that deny the United States a permanent military presence ashore in the Gulf region could easily be invoked to deny the United States agreed access to facilities in the event of crisis. The problem is compounded by antagonisms among states that have concluded access agreements with the United States, the most notable example being Kenya and Somalia.[97] The prospect of U.S. military assistance to Somalia in exchange for access to Berbera not only has alarmed Kenya but also threatens to entangle the United States in Somalia's attempt to wrest the Ogaden from Ethiopia. It is perhaps not unrealistic to assume that, among those states which have granted the United States contingent access to U.S. military facilities, the desire to assist U.S. military power was not the principal motivation.

---

[94]According to sources in the Department of Defense, identifiable military construction costs associated with planned U.S. improvements in facilities to which the United States has been granted access in Oman, Kenya, and Somalia will total $374 million for the period of fiscal years 1981-1983.

[95]In the summer of 1980, a USAF F-4 Phantom jet squadron was deployed to Egypt for several weeks, where it conducted joint exercises with the Egyptian Air Force. In November 1980, an RDF-earmarked battalion of the U.S. Army's 101st Airborne (Air Assault) Division and an Air Force detachment were airlifted to Egypt in a logistical exercise.

[96]Testimony of Under-Secretary of Defense Robert Komer, *Hearings, op. cit.,* Part 1, p. 435.

[97]Jay Ross, "U.S. Arms Accord with Somalia Alarms Rival Neighbor Kenya," *Washington Post,* October 20, 1980.

5. Weaknesses

It is apparent that the present and prospective Rapid Deployment Force envisaged by the Department of Defense successfully addresses few of the problems confronting U.S. military intervention in the Persian Gulf. Most planned increases in strategic mobility, desirable though they are, fall far short of ensuring the timely arrival of sufficient force either to preempt Soviet intervention or to defeat Soviet forces in place; moreover, they are based upon the presumption that forces to be moved will be ready. In any event, early arriving RDF ground forces would lack the organic tactical mobility and firepower to deal effectively with Soviet forces or Soviet-model client armies. Another weakness of the RDF is its dependence on a politically tenuous shore-based logistical infrastructure—a dependence dictated by the size and composition of contemplated intervention forces and evident in the search for contingent access to military facilities in the region. The potentially perverse consequences of this dependence are compounded by the no less politically tenuous presumption of a benign landing environment, a presumption manifest both in the character of RDF-related strategic mobility initiatives and in the absence of expanded forcible-entry capabilities. Overshadowing all these deficiencies is a command apparatus reflecting not the exacting demands of combined operations but rather interservice rivalry for possession of the rapid deployment mission.

Insufficient Strategic Mobility

There is no doubt that the airlift and sealift enhancement initiatives associated with the RDF contribute to strategic mobility, and that strategic mobility is an essential attribute of any U.S. intervention force devised for the Persian Gulf. Yet the initiatives do not fully serve the RDF's twin goals of being able to *preempt* Soviet intervention or local aggression in the Gulf and to *reinforce* adequately a commitment once made. The root of the problem lies in the decision to form the RDF from forces based almost entirely in the United States, half a world away from the Persian Gulf. The decision severely reduces the possibility of preempting an adversary already in or near the Gulf, since the timely delivery of forces from the United States would require not only a sizable amount of warning time[98]

---

[98]According to Pentagon planners, at least *one month* of warning would be required "to be able to move a force large enough to have some chance of dissuading an aggressor." Richard Halloran, "Gaps in Training and Equipment Hinder Rapid Deployment Force," *New York Times,* September 26, 1980.

but also a political willingness to act in a "provocative" manner during a crisis. Even ample warning and an early decision to intervene, however, are not likely to be enough. The greater proximity of larger Soviet forces, particularly the Soviet Army's strategically mobile and tactically capable airborne divisions, more than offsets the ability of planned increases in U.S. strategic airlift and sealift capabilities to deploy a multi-division force to the Gulf within three weeks of a decision to intervene;[99] the planned increases are not likely to deter an adversary *already* capable of deploying substantial forces to the region within a matter of days.

The conclusion is thus inescapable that the only U.S. forces likely to be immediately available in time of need are those *already* prepositioned in the Gulf region. If the United States is to succeed in preempting Soviet intervention or local aggression, it must do so with forces forward-deployed or prepositioned in the Gulf region. A sizable and visible U.S. military presence in the region has undoubted deterrent value. More to the point, reliance on forward-deployed naval forces and prepositioned ground forces, by virtue of their proximity to potential trouble spots, reduces the requirement for warning time; additionally, their utilization in a crisis would not carry with it the degree of escalatory risk associated with the mobilization and transfer of forces based in the United States. In this regard, the value of smaller RDF forces prepositioned afloat in the Indian Ocean far exceeds that of larger RDF forces withheld in the United States.

The ability to reinforce any initial U.S. commitment in the Gulf is essential, and it does require ensuring the strategic mobility of the U.S.-based portion of the RDF. On the other hand, the ability to reinforce is of little use if forward-deployed forces initially committed to combat are destroyed because of inadequate strength or structure. Thus, the principal strategic mobility issue is not the wisdom of prepositioning a U.S. Marine division afloat in the Indian Ocean, but whether that division and supporting naval and carrier-based aviation forces are sufficient in both size and capabilities to deal effectively with likely threats, at least until reinforcements arrive from the United States.

Inadequate Tactical Mobility

One of the more disconcerting aspects of the RDF has been the apparent lack of recognition on the part of the Department of Defense that current strategically mobile ground forces possess little staying power on the

---

[99]George C. Wilson, "Outlook Grim in a War for Mideast Oil," *Washington Post,* October 28, 1980.

battlefield against the heavy, fully mechanized forces characteristic of the Soviet Army and of Soviet-model client armies in the Gulf region. In forming a pool of general forces for the RDF, the Pentagon has been understandably attracted by the inherent strategic mobility of light, foot-mobile infantry formations like the Army's 82nd and 101st Airborne divisions and the Marine Corps' amphibious brigades. Having defined the "problem" of intervention in the Gulf almost exclusively in terms of strategic mobility, Pentagon planners accordingly have ignored the fact that strategic mobility in U.S. ground forces has always been purchased at the expense of the tactical mobility and firepower needed to survive against an armored or mechanized adversary (see discussion in Chapter 3). Indeed, even though the concept of maritime prepositioning provides the opportunity to place a heavy division in the Indian Ocean, the decision has been made instead to place the equipment of a Marine division aboard the MPS.

With the exception of the Army's 24th (Mechanized) Infantry Division and 194th Armored Brigade, none of the ground force units earmarked for rapid deployment possesses sufficient tanks, self-propelled artillery, and armored personnel carriers to meet even minimum tactical mobility and firepower requirements against a fully mechanized opponent operating in terrain often tailor-made for armored maneuver warfare. The Marine division's equipment to be prepositioned afloat in the Indian Ocean by fiscal 1987 will include only about 150 tanks, 300 armored troop carriers, and 40 self-propelled guns—less than half the numbers of these weapons to be found in a Soviet-model mechanized division.

In short, while unmechanized infantry may be able to get to the Gulf faster, its prospects for survival against mechanized forces are not encouraging. Foot infantry's traditional reliance on tactical airpower and on assault and troop-carrying helicopters to offset deficiencies in firepower and tactical mobility is not likely to succeed in the Persian Gulf, given the proximity of Soviet land-based aviation, to say nothing of the dense tactical air defenses characteristic of both Soviet and indigenous Soviet-model armies in the region. Continued confidence in the ability of "flying" artillery to make good the dearth of guns on the ground would seem to dismiss one of the central lessons of the Arab-Israeli War of 1973.

Dependence on a Shore-Based Logistical Infrastructure

The character of modern, high-technology U.S. ground and tactical air forces, with their low ratios of combat to support personnel, makes it virtually impossible to sustain any prolonged military intervention in the Gulf in the absence of a large, shore-based logistical infrastructure. This would certainly be the case in intervention involving two or three U.S. Army divisions and three or four USAF tactical fighter wings. Illustrative of the problem was the deployment to Egypt in the summer of 1980 of a single squadron of 12 F-4 Phantom fighter bombers, a deployment accompanied by no fewer than 300 support personnel, for whom temporary housing had to be constructed. Deployment of even the light, 15,700-man 82nd Airborne Division to the Gulf would entail the movement and establishment ashore of some 11,000 support personnel.[100]

Firm possession of an adequate shore-based logistical infrastructure is not a problem in Europe and Northeast Asia, where U.S. forces are already in place and enjoy secure logistical arrangements with powerful and reliable allies. In the Persian Gulf, however, the United States enjoys no secure military access ashore; any shore-based logistical infrastructure could be maintained only at the sufferance of politically unstable host governments, and there can never be any guarantee of access in a crisis. Present arrangements for contingent access to facilities in Kenya, Oman, and Somalia, while desirable, could be revoked without warning; they would certainly count for nothing in the event of an anti-Western revolution of the kind that toppled the Shah of Iran. Indeed, the very establishment during a crisis of the kind of sprawling logistical empire ashore that characterized U.S. intervention in Vietnam is likely to excite, as it did in Vietnam, precisely the anti-Western violence intervention is designed to suppress.

What is really at issue is the style of intervention implicit in the size and composition of forces earmarked for the RDF. Large-scale intervention relying heavily on U.S. Army units and on land-based (USAF) tactical airpower—as opposed to sea-based carrier aviation and Marine Corps units—places prospects for success or failure largely in the hands of those in the Persian Gulf who exercise sovereignty over territory without which intervention could not be supported. To stake the success or failure of an intervention force on the momentary political whims of local regimes in the Gulf serves the security interests of neither the United States nor the Western world as a whole.

Insufficient Forcible-Entry Capabilities

As noted in the preceding chapter, the efficacy of all of the strategic mobility initiatives associated with the RDF—the CX, Maritime Prepositioning Ship, and various airlift and sealift enhancement programs—is

---

[100]The 82nd contains some 15,700 personnel. Yet, as shown in Table 3, deployment of the division to the Persian Gulf would entail the movement of 27,500 personnel.

limited exclusively to a benign landing environment. Unarmed strategic transport aircraft and cargo ships cannot force their way into defended airfields and ports, or onto beaches. Defended entry points must first be "cleared" by either amphibious or airborne assault forces (or both) and the latter cannot long survive in a hostile ground environment unless relieved by other friendly ground forces.

The issue is whether the Department of Defense's presumption of an uncontested landing environment—implicit in the RDF-related strategic mobility initiatives—is justified. To be sure, one can envisage a number of scenarios in which a host nation in firm control of its ports and airfields would invite U.S. forces to come ashore. Yet one also can envisage situations in which either Soviet or hostile indigenous forces had seized possession of such facilities before the United States decided to act or, having decided, before RDF forces could be brought to bear in the area. Certainly, the Iranian government in April 1980 did not invite the United States to rescue its diplomatic personnel being held hostage in Tehran.

In short, there seems to be little justification for the view that the RDF could expect a "free ride" ashore in the Persian Gulf. On the contrary, it can be argued that the Department of Defense's comparative inattention to reconstituting traditional U.S. forcible entry capabilities as part and parcel of a rapid deployment force would serve in a crisis to encourage preemptive conquest or destruction of ports and airfields by potential adversaries. An intervention force known to be dependent on a friendly reception is likely not to get one. As Marine Corps Commandant Robert H. Barrow repeatedly stressed during Congressional Hearings on the RDF.

The Maritime Prepositioning Program is a means of enhancing our strategic mobility only. It is not a substitute for United States ability to project power into a hostile environment. It is essential to emphasize that the Maritime Prepositioned force can be brought to bear only in a non-hostile scenario or after a suitable port and airfield complex is secured by other means—such as amphibious assault. Unquestionably, the prepositioned ships will provide us a capability to build up an amphibious assault force rapidly after suitable reception facilities have been uncovered, but we must not be lulled into the perception that commercially designed and crewed ships are substitutes for war ships. The level of the amphibious fleet is already below that considered necessary by the Joint Chiefs of Staff to carry out our national strategy with reasonable assurances of success.[101]

The question of how much forcible-entry capability is enough is difficult to answer. A strong case can be made, however, that the present level of amphibious shipping—the lowest since *before* World War II—is insuffi-

---

[101]*Hearings, op. cit.,* Part 2, p. 857.

cient, certainly for a major contingency in the Persian Gulf. As noted by General Barrow, the current level of amphibious shipping, upon which any assault against a hostile shoreline depends, is less than one-half the planning force requirement specified in 1976 by the Joint Chiefs of Staff.[102] The Navy's present 64 amphibious vessels are capable of lifting only one of the Marine Corps' three divisions, and since the ships are scattered throughout the Navy's various fleets, a minimum of 30 days would be required to assemble in one place the shipping necessary to mount a division-sized assault.

The precipitate decline in levels of amphibious shipping during the past two decades has been accompanied by an even more dramatic drop in naval gunfire support, the only all-weather fire support available to amphibious forces during the assault. Since 1964, for example, the total number of gun barrels—3-inch or larger—mounted on active naval vessels has declined by 70 percent (from almost 1,300 to less than 400), reducing the total salvo weight by over 80 percent.[103] The possibility of recalling to active service one or more *Iowa*-class battleships, which was seriously considered by the Congress in 1980, was opposed by the Department of Defense on the grounds that the Navy would be incapable of manning the vessels.[104]

To sum up, present U.S. forcible-entry capabilities do not appear sufficient either for deterrence or defense in the Persian Gulf, unless the United States is prepared to confine any significant military intervention in the region to circumstances in which forcible entry is not required. In fact, the very absence of planned increases in such capabilities, which have been declining steadily since the Korean War, serves to invite military preemption of an RDF all too dependent on peaceful ports and airfields.

Divided Command

Perhaps the greatest single weakness of the RDF, however, is its divided command, compounded by divided military jurisdiction in the Indian Ocean and the Persian Gulf between the U.S. European and Pacific Commands. A successful combined operation requires a single, cen-

---

[102]The present level of amphibious shipping is capable of lifting 1.15 Marine Amphibious Forces (division-wing teams); the planning force requirement specified by the JCS is for 2.33 MAFs.

[103]Martin Binkin and Jeffrey Record, *Where Does the Marine Corps Go From Here?* (Washington, D.C.: Brookings Institution, 1976), p. 27.

[104]See testimony of Deputy Secretary of Defense W. Graham Claytor, Jr., in *Hearings, op. cit.*, Part 2, p. 1131.

tralized command possessing unchallenged authority over pre-operation planning and forces earmarked for the operation, as well as authority over the execution of the operation itself. Such was the case with respect to the great combined operations in Europe and the Pacific during World War II, and during the subsequent conflict in Korea.

In the case of the RDF, however, responsibility for planning and the training of forces in peacetime has been assigned to one organization—the U.S. Readiness Command—while responsibility for the execution of operations in wartime has been vested in another—the Rapid Deployment Joint Task Force. In essence, RDJTF Commander P. X. Kelley will lead into battle forces whose availability is beyond his control, and he will have to fight the battle with operational plans devised largely by others. Not even joint-service training in peacetime is guaranteed, since REDCOM has no jurisdiction over Navy and Marine Corps forces, and only limited authority over U.S. Air Force participation. Moreover, once RDF forces arrive in the Persian Gulf region, they will be subject, depending on their location, to two conflicting U.S. regional commands: outside the Persian Gulf they will be under the ultimate control of the U.S. Pacific Command based in Hawaii; inside the Gulf or ashore on the Gulf's adjacent land masses (Iran and the Arabian peninsula) they will fall under the jurisdiction of the U.S. European Command.

It does not require genius to discern that the cluttered and fragmented command relationships surrounding the RDF, which are to a large extent the product of interservice rivalry for the rapid deployment mission, are fertile ground for military defeat. One has only to recall the disaster that befell the U.S. hostage rescue mission in the Iranian desert, a disaster attributable as much to confused command as it was to technical failure. The scene at "Desert 1," as described in a study commissioned by the Joint Chiefs of Staff, could be illustrative on a small scale of future U.S. military intervention in the Gulf involving the RDF.

As complex and difficult as the Desert One scenario was, it had not been fully rehearsed. A training exercise at the western training area conducted on 13-14 April with two C-130s and four H-53s was used to validate the Desert One concept. Perhaps because the scope and complexity of Desert One was not replicated in a full-dress rehearsal, the plan for this desert rendezvous was soft. There was no identifiable command post for the on-scene commander; a staff and runners were not anticipated; backup rescue radios were not available until the third C-130 arrived; and, lastly, key personnel and those with critical functions were not identified for ease of recognition. For example, when the Desert One on-scene commander's name surfaced during the post-mission interviews with helicopter pilots, they stated that, in some cases, they did not know or recognize the authority of those giving orders at Desert One. In this regard, instructions to evacuate helicopters and board the C-130s had to be questioned to determine the identity of those giving the orders to establish their proper authority.[105]

The weaknesses of the RDF identified in this chapter, grave though they are, are not insurmountable. Overcoming the RDF's present deficiencies, however, will require fundamental alterations in both the concept of military intervention in the Gulf and in the character of the RDF itself. Those alterations are the subject of the following chapter.

---

[105]Joint Chiefs of Staff, *Rescue Mission Report* (Washington, D.C.: August 1980), p. 50.

6. Solutions

In the author's judgment, the deficiencies of the present Rapid Deployment Force can be overcome only through its replacement by *a small, agile, tactically capable intervention force that is based at and supplied from the sea, governed by a single, unified command, and supported by expanded sea power, especially forcible-entry capabilities.* Such an intervention force would stress *quality* at the expense of size; *immediate responsiveness* at the expense of delayed augmentation from the United States; *sea-based power projection capabilities* at the expense of air-transported Army forces and land-based tactical air power; and *logistical self-sufficiency* at the expense of dependence on facilities ashore. The present composition and capabilities of the RDF are the product less of impartial military judgment than they are of the bureaucratic desire of each service for at least a "fair share" of the rapid deployment mission. As such, the present RDF can and should be replaced by a *new variant of the Navy-Fleet Marine Force "team," utilizing tried and tested organizational structures and operational doctrines associated with the successful projection of power from sea to shore.*

Specifically, the author proposes:

(1) the transfer of the primary responsibility for the rapid deployment mission to the U.S. Marine Corps, together with the establishment, in the form of a new, 5th Fleet, of a unified U.S. command with jurisdiction over the whole Indian Ocean and Persian Gulf region;

(2) an expansion in planned increases in strategic mobility through greater reliance on maritime prepositioning, with the object of strengthening the forward-deployed component of the RDF;

(3) the creation of genuine tactical agility for RDF ground forces through acquisition of lightweight armored fighting vehicles and adoption of a maneuver warfare operational doctrine;

(4) the elimination of RDF dependence on a shore-based logistical infrastructure through development of sea-based logistical capabilities to supply and perform even second-echelon maintenance for RDF forces committed ashore; and

(5) an increase in forcible entry capabilities through increases in present levels of amphibious shipping and naval gunfire support.

Transferring the Rapid Deployment Mission to the Marines

Many of the command problems currently plaguing the RDF could be eliminated by transferring *responsibility* for the rapid deployment mission to a single service. Doing so—as opposed to parceling out bits and pieces of it to several services—would not only remove the mission from the arena of debilitating interservice rivalry but also serve to integrate, under a single organization, the critical functions of planning, training, and execution of operations.

Given the peculiar obstacles to and requirements for successful U.S. military intervention in the Persian Gulf, a strong case can be made for transferring the mission to the U.S. Marine Corps. Leaving aside the fact that a Marine Corps general already has been appointed to command the Rapid Deployment Joint Task Force, the lack of any real prospect for establishing an operationally significant peacetime U.S. military presence ashore in the Persian Gulf region (to say nothing of the potential unwanted political and military entanglements such a presence would invite) virtually dictates primary reliance on sea power, and especially on the kind of sea-based capabilities to project power ashore long associated with the Marine Corps.

The Marine Corps is the sole repository of U.S. amphibious assault capabilities, an essential component of any credible U.S. intervention force in the Persian Gulf. Moreover, unlike the Army, which must rely on another service for tactical air support, the Corps has its own air arm, not only compatible with carriers and other sea-based air platforms but also highly integrated with both carrier-based naval aviation and Marine ground forces. In short, in contrast to the Army, the Corps' principal competitor for bureaucratic control of the rapid deployment mission, the Marine Corps is fully compatible with sea power—the necessary foundation of a U.S. military presence in those areas of the world where U.S. forces are not stationed ashore. There is also the Corps' longstanding history of successful expeditionary operations in the Third World, and its record, as the nation's recognized "force in readiness," of being the "first to fight."

The comparative attractiveness of sea-based ground forces for the kinds of tasks entailed in the rapid deployment mission has long been recognized. As B. H. Liddell Hart observed in 1960,

While it is desirable to have an airborne force, which enables quicker intervention where its use is possible, it is essential to have a marine force, and better that this should be the bigger of the two. For the bigger, it is the more possible because a strategic deployment wide enough and strong enough to ensure early

70

and effective intervention wherever there is a blaze and before it spreads. An amphibious force of modern type, operating from the sea and equipped with helicopters, is free from dependence on airfields, beaches, ports and land-bases with all their logistical and political complications. The use of an airborne force or of any land-based force is a more irrevocable step, since its commitment is more definite and its withdrawal more difficult. A self-contained and sea-based amphibious force, of which the U.S. Marine Corps is the prototype, is the best kind of fire extinguisher, because of its flexibility, reliability, logistic simplicity and relative economy.[106]

Transferring responsibility for the rapid deployment mission to the Marine Corps could be accomplished simply by a Congressional act declaring the Corps to be the Rapid Deployment Force without prejudice to the Corps' more traditional missions, many of which (e.g., amphibious assault) already lend themselves to the rapid deployment mission.

Such a legislative declaration would not exclude the potential participation of non-Marine formations in a Persian Gulf contingency, but would make it clear that their participation would be subject to the operational command of designated Marine Corps authority. Intervention could well require the participation of organizations (e.g., the U.S. Military Airlift Command) and forces (e.g., U.S. Army airborne, Special Forces, or Ranger units) outside the jurisdiction of the Marine Corps and its parent organization, the Department of the Navy. Once the decision to intervene has been made, however, such organizations and forces must be subordinated to the operational command of the designated Marine Corps authority for the RDF; and in peacetime they must be made available to that authority for planning and training purposes.

Indeed, with respect to land forces in general, it can be and has been persuasively argued that a formal geographic "division of ground combat labor" between the Marine Corps and Army is implicit in the distinctive capabilities separating the two services.[107] Since World War I, the central focus in Army force planning has been a major war in Europe against one or more large, modern continental adversaries; it is a continuing focus reflected in the Army's preference for heavy formations, whose limited strategic mobility has been offset by the deployment in Europe of some five of the Army's 16 active divisions and the prepositioning there of equipment for an additional five divisions.[108] In contrast are the Marine

[106]B.H. Liddell Hart, "Marines and Strategy," *The Marine Corps Gazette,* July 1960, p. 31.

[107]Senator Gary Hart and Robert Taft, Jr., *White Paper on Defense: A Modern Military Strategy for the United States* (Washington, D.C., 1978).

[108]An implicit admission of the structural unsuitability of most Army divisions for the rapid deployment mission is evident in the Army's present attempt, utilizing the 9th Infantry

Corps' three division-wing teams (known as Marine Amphibious Forces, each containing a ground division and tactical air wing), none of which is "tied down" in Europe or in any other specific location overseas. Fleet Marine Forces (the three MAFs) are regarded by the Department of Defense as strategically mobile strike forces to be committed anywhere in the world on the basis of need.

In the author's opinion, the Army's responsibilities should be confined to contingencies in areas where U.S. ground forces are already prepositioned ashore (Europe and Korea), with the Marine Corps' responsibilities restricted to those areas where they are not. Such a division of labor, which seems implicit in the transfer of the rapid deployment mission to the Marine Corps, would require the Corps to divest itself of residual NATO missions, most of which can and should be performed by the Army.[109]

In terms of size, the 186,000-man Marine Corps is more than sufficient to fulfill the requirements of any Persian Gulf contingency, except those which the Corps and the Army together could not meet (e.g., a full-scale Soviet invasion of Iran). In terms of capabilities, the limited tactical mobility and firepower of Marine ground forces can be overcome by an expansion or acceleration of research and development and procurement programs already underway (see discussion below). The Corps' lack of airborne assault capabilities is a problem that can be solved either by the establishment of a proper command and control relationship between the Corps and the Army's 18th Airborne Corps (composed of the 82nd and 101st Airborne divisions), or by the transfer of the airborne mission itself to the Corps.[110] The latter would establish the Corps as the sole repository of U.S. forcible entry capabilities and thereby simplify com-

---

Division as a test instrument, to devise a strategically *and* tactically mobile formation based on lightweight armor and other new technologies. See Richard Halloran, "Army Begins Experiments to Design New Mobile Strike Force," *The Oregonian,* December 22, 1980.

[109]Marine Corps ground forces, which are structured and equipped primarily for amphibious warfare, are unsuited for inland combat in Central Europe against Warsaw Pact forces. The two Marine Amphibious Forces (the 1st and 2nd MAFs), currently earmarked for NATO contingencies, should therefore be removed from the Strategic Reserve of the Supreme Allied Commander, Europe. Even the prospect of successful amphibious assaults along NATO's Northern and Southern Flanks has diminished in the face of the growing reach of Soviet land-based aviation. Current Department of Defense plans to preposition equipment for a Marine brigade in Norway are predicated on the arrival by air of the brigade in Norway before the outbreak of hostilities; as such, the ground defense of Norway can and should be handled by a combination of Norwegian and U.S. Army forces.

[110]Martin Binkin and Jeffrey Record, *Where Does the Marine Corps Go from Here?* (Washington, D.C.: Brookings Institution, 1976), pp. 78-81.

mand and control of operations involving both airborne and amphibious assaults.

Removing the RDJTF from the overlordship of REDCOM offers no solution per se to the problem of command: the real issue is whether the RDF should be primarily a sea-based or a land-dependent force. For example, transferring the RDJTF from REDCOM to the U.S. European Command, an option reportedly under serious consideration by the Joint Chiefs of Staff in February 1981, would do little other than shift the locus of interservice rivalry for the rapid deployment mission from Florida to Europe. EUCOM is an inland-warfare-oriented command, dominated by the U.S. Army and Air Force, and already overburdened by the demanding tasks posed by burgeoning Soviet military power in Europe.

Establishing a Unified Command in the Indian Ocean and Persian Gulf

A companion measure to the establishment of the Marine Corps as the RDF would be the creation of a single unified command in the Indian Ocean and Persian Gulf region, thus eliminating the present jurisdictional division of the area between the U.S. European and Pacific commands. The vehicle for unification would be a new, 5th Fleet, whose commander-in-chief—a naval officer—would exercise operational control over all U.S. military forces in the region, including that portion of Marine RDF forces maintained on station in the Indian Ocean. The relationship between the Commander-in-Chief, Indian Ocean/Persian Gulf, and the Deputy Commander for Rapid Deployment Forces—a Marine officer—would be identical to that which since World War II has governed the relationship between Marine and naval forces in amphibious operations: the Navy would retain command authority over intervention operations until intervention forces were firmly established ashore, at which point that authority would pass to the Marine Corps.

Substantial U.S. naval forces, drawn from both the Mediterranean and Western Pacific, already have been deployed in the Indian Ocean for an indefinite term, as have logistics ships containing equipment for a Marine Amphibious Brigade. Thus, a U.S. fleet in the region already exists. What is needed is a commensurate institutionalization of command authority that would further the conduct of combined operations.

An alternative to the creation of a new unified command in the Indian Ocean would be simply to extend the operational jurisdiction of the U.S. Pacific Command to the Persian Gulf, Red Sea, and adjacent land masses. This option is attractive for a number of reasons, not the least of which is the maritime orientation of the command and the presence of substantial Marine Corps forces within it.

Increasing Strategic Mobility

Present programs to enhance the strategic mobility of the RDF could be augmented by greater reliance on maritime prepositioning than currently anticipated. As we have seen, the prepositioning of forces afloat in the Indian Ocean is more cost-effective than "lifting" U.S.-based forces to the region. Prepositioned forces, moreover, provided a much more responsive defense to potential threats, a critical attribute in deterring preemption by hostile forces.

In the author's judgment, serious consideration should be given to the maritime prepositioning of more than one division in the Indian Ocean. The prepositioning of equipment and combat consumables for one and two-third divisions (five brigades) or even two divisions (six brigades) would not only strengthen short-warning intervention capabilities but also reduce comparatively costly investment in strategic airlift and sealift forces associated with RDF forces in the United States. Alternatively, one division could be prepositioned in the Indian Ocean (as planned), with a second, fully supported by fast sealift vessels, retained in the United States.

This is not to suggest that additional strategic lift capabilities are unnecessary. There is a limit to the amount of military power that can be prepositioned afloat in the Indian Ocean, and a major contingency might well require timely reinforcement from the United States. Expansion in strategic lift capabilities is desirable, although the comparative cost-effectiveness of strategic airlift (especially the proposed CX) argues strongly for allocating the bulk of additional "strategic lift" dollars to *sea* lift programs.

Increasing Tactical Mobility

Primary reliance on unmechanized, foot-mobile infantry formations—including the Marine brigade currently prepositioned afloat in the Indian Ocean—deprives RDF ground forces of the tactical mobility and firepower that could prove essential in combat against larger, mechanized potential adversaries in the Gulf region. Endowing those forces with the requisite tactical mobility can be accomplished through the acquisition of lightweight armored fighting vehicles that could be utilized by both prepositioned and U.S.-based ground forces of the RDF.[111] The primary

---

[111]See James F. Hollingsworth and Allan T. Wood, "The Light Armored Corps—A Strategic Necessity," *Armed Forces Journal,* January 1980; and Jeffrey Record, "Why Plan Rapid Deployment of the Wrong Kind of Force?," *Washington Star,* February 3, 1980.

advantage of lightweight armor is that it provides a high degree of tactical mobility and firepower without imposing the penalty of strategic immobility associated with standard 40- to 60-ton main battle tanks (like the U.S. Army's 60-ton XM-1) and 20- to 30-ton infantry fighting vehicles (like the Army's new XM-2). As noted by one senior Marine Corps officer, lightweight armor would permit the RDF to "be light enough to get [to the Persian Gulf in time] but heavy enough to win."[112]

The inherent benefits of lightweight armor for Persian Gulf contingencies have long been apparent in the Marine Corps, which, through an initiative known as the Light Armored Vehicle (LAV) program, is currently testing a number of extant foreign and domestic vehicle designs for acquisition in the near term. Candidate vehicles include the French wheeled AMX-10RC; the British Scorpion light tank; the Swiss Piranha armored personnel carrier; the Brazilian Urutu APC: and the Cadillac-Gage V-150 Commando weapons carrier. In the author's view, the LAV program should be accelerated with the aim of acquiring an interim force of lightweight armored vehicles at the earliest possible date.

As a long-term solution to the problem of insufficient tactical mobility, the Corps is developing a new, small, 14-ton "tankette" known as the Mobile Protected Weapons System (MPWS). The MPWS relies primarily on agility and a low silhouette for protection, and mounts a revolutionary rapid-fire, high-velocity 75-millimeter gun possessing a lethality comparable to the standard 105-millimeter tank gun.[113] Scheduled for initial production in the mid-1980s, the MPWS, whose chassis and power plant could form the basis for a set of companion vehicles,[114] is far more compatible with present and planned U.S. airlift and sealift capabilities than the Army's armored fighting vehicles. For example, the Army's XM-1 main battle tank is too large and heavy to be carried by either the C-141 or the tactical C-130 transport; only two can be carried by the mammoth C-5A. In contrast, as many as six MPWS could be lifted by the C-5A; three by the C-141; and two by the C-130.[115] The MPWS is, moreover, helicopter-transportable, which allows it to be moved quickly from ship to shore or, once on land, to avoid negotiating intervening terrain between distant objectives.

---

[112]Testimony of Major General Alfred M. Gray, Director, Development Center, Marine Corps Combat Development and Education Command, in *Hearings, op. cit.,* Part 6, p. 3342.

[113]Lawrence B. Fitzmorris, "Experimenting for Tomorrow's Combat Vehicles," *Army Research, Development and Acquisition Magazine,* November-December 1979.

[114]The MPWS family of vehicles envisaged by Marine Corps force planners include command and control vehicles, armored personnel carriers, mortar carriers, air defense artillery platforms, and recovery vehicles. For a detailed description of the LAV, MPWS, and related programs, see *Hearings, op. cit.,* pp. 3343-3359.

[115]*Ibid.,* Part 1, p. 456.

Like the LAV program, the MPWS program should be accelerated, although priority should be accorded to the creation of an interim force based on existing designs already in production.

Possession of the means of tactical mobility, however, is not enough. Means must be married to an operational doctrine—maneuver warfare—that confers upon smaller, lighter forces (early-arriving RDF contingents) the ability to defeat larger, heavier forces (Soviet or regional Soviet-model forces). The concept of maneuver warfare and its relation to potential future Marine Corps combat operations in the Persian Gulf was cogently and convincingly treated in a recent article by William S. Lind, a noted land warfare expert and student of maneuver.[116]

Maneuver warfare refers to an overall concept or "style" of warfare. It has an opposite, the firepower-attrition style.

Firepower-attrition is warfare on the model of Verdun in World War I, a mutual casualty inflicting and absorbing contest where the goal is a favorable exchange rate. The conflict is more physical than mental. Efforts focus on the tactical level with goals set in terms of terrain. Defenses tend to be linear ("forward defense"), attacks frontal, battles set-piece and movement preplanned and slow.

In contrast, maneuver war is warfare on the model of Genghis Khan, the German blitzkrieg and almost all Israeli campaigns. The goal is destruction of the enemy's vital cohesion—disruption—not piece-by-piece physical destruction. The objective is the enemy's mind not his body. The principal tool is moving forces into unexpected places at surprisingly high speeds. Firepower is a servant of maneuver, used to create openings in enemy defenses and, when necessary, to annihilate the remnants of his forces after their cohesion has been shattered.

Maneuver conflict is more psychological than physical. Effort focuses more on the operational than on the tactical level. The goal is set in terms of destroying the enemy's forces not seizing terrain seen a priori as "key." A defender places only a "tripwire" forward and relies on counterattacks into the flanks and rear of enemy penetrations. "One up and two back" is the rule. Attacks ooze through and around enemy defenses. Battles are usually meeting engagements. Rates of advance are high. Movement is constant, irregular in direction and timing and responsive to fleeting opportunities.

A key to understanding maneuver war is to realize that not all movement is maneuver. Maneuver is relational movement. Maneuver is not a matter simply of moving or even of moving rapidly. Maneuver means moving and acting consistently more rapidly than the opponent.

. . . .

---

[116]William S. Lind, "Defining Maneuver Warfare for the Marine Corps," *Marine Corps Gazette*, March 1980, pp. 55-58.

Maneuver war relates directly to the probable main mission of the Corps during the remainder of this century, supporting the United States' friends in the Third World. Despite the current Administration's fixation on NATO, Europe is becoming relatively less important to United States' interests and non-European areas, developed and less developed, more important. Japan is now the United States' largest single overseas trading partner. America's vital interest in areas rich in raw materials, especially petroleum, is well known. The increasing economic vitality of parts of Latin America, especially Brazil, suggests our interests in that area may become more important.

In many potential Third World scenarios, the Marine Corps faces an opponent superior in numbers and materiel—possibly quality as well as quantity of materiel. For example, if we consider the possibility of Marine Corps intervention to assist Saudi Arabia against an attack by Iraq, we see Iraq has an army of 180,000 men, compared to only 80,000 for Saudi Arabia (including the Saudi National Guard). Iraqi forces include four armored and two mechanized divisions. Equipment includes T-62 and AMX-30 tanks, BMPs, multiple rocket launchers and ZSU-23-4 anti-aircraft guns—equipment equal or superior to that possessed by Marines. The supporting air force has 339 combat aircraft, including modern MIG-23s, SU-20s, and Mirage F-1s. While Saudi equipment is also modern, quantities are smaller. Operational effectiveness also may be less.

Maneuver warfare would offer a Marine amphibious force (MAF) the best chance in assisting Saudi forces to victory. An attrition contest between well-equipped Iraqi mechanized divisions and a single MAF would not be promising. The need is for a force which, although small, can wage maneuver warfare in support of an ally who probably cannot, against an opponent who probably cannot.

Indeed, the force multiplier effect of maneuver warfare should be more striking against a Third World opponent. While Third World armies may be large, well-equipped and competent at operating their weapons systems, they are likely to be tactically and operationally inflexible. Third World nations can produce some highly competent officers and planners, as the Egyptians demonstrated in the canal crossing in 1973. But they are not likely to have many such officers, and flexibility may be lacking in field forces. The impact of maneuver warfare, with its emphasis on speed, surprise and the creation of unexpected situations, could be devastating. Such has been Israel's experience in several wars with her Third World neighbors. However good the prewar planning and set-piece operations of the Arabs, the Israeli maneuver style of warfare triumphed dramatically once the situation became fluid. The reason was not that Israeli equipment was better or that Israeli troops were more courageous, but that Israeli field forces showed great flexibility. Their opponents did not.

It is sometimes mistakenly thought that maneuver warfare automatically means armored warfare. To be sure, foot infantry cannot fight effective maneuver war in open terrain. But in rugged terrain, maneuver concepts apply fully to infantry warfare. Indeed, maneuver war was first manifest in the West in this century during World War I by German foot infantry in so-called infiltration, "von Hutier" or "soft-spot" tactics. The World War II Blitzkrieg differed little in concept from these early infiltration tactics, merely substituting tanks for storm troops and achieving the higher rates of advance permitted by mechanization. Infiltration tactics may offer as much potential to Marine foot infantry as to future Marine mechanized units.

Changes will be required in the Marine Corps if it is to fight maneuver warfare effectively. Maneuver doctrine must be developed and disseminated. Marine foot infantry may have to become lighter if it is to fight maneuver warfare effectively in appropriate terrain. Mechanized forces must be formed for open terrain, not based on heavy tanks and tracked infantry fighting vehicles which restrict strategic mobility but on a family of lightweight, probably wheeled combat vehicles. To provide strategic responsiveness, equipment for substantial mechanized units should be prepositioned at sea in potential trouble areas, probably on roll-on, roll-off (RO-RO) ships. Some arms, especially artillery, may require expansion.

But unlike the Army, the Marine Corps can develop a strategically responsive force to fight maneuver war in Third World areas. Bound as it is to airlift and to land prepositioning, the Army cannot quickly move mechanized forces over strategic distances. The Army, like the Marine Corps, could preposition equipment at sea. But then the Army would become another Marine Corps, and few force planners think we need two.

A shift to maneuver warfare offers a major challenge to Marines. But it is an exciting challenge, especially for company and field grade officers. In maneuver warfare, the responsibility placed on company and field grades increases dramatically. The key to maintaining a rapid observation-decision-action cycle is to make all decisions on the lowest possible level, the company and battalion level. This is one of the fundamental principles of the German army and is central to their concept of mission orders tactics (Auftragstaktik). Mission orders tactics require company and field grade officers to understand the concepts of maneuver war and of the operation in which they are engaged. Only through a solid conceptual understanding can they hope to make the right decisions on their own as events occur in the field.

There is no question Marines can meet the challenge. By adopting a maneuver concept of war, they can give the United States the capability it needs to defend its vital interests outside Europe. And by performing that task, the Marine Corps can assure itself a solid mission of unquestionable value.

Developing a Sea-Based Logistical Infrastructure

The Marine Corps has been criticized in recent years, with some justice, for thinking too much of taking a beach and too little about the subsequent campaign beyond the beach. Measures such as the creation of distinctive mechanized units, equipped with lightweight armored vehicles, are directed at this deficiency.

Ironically, it can be said with equal justice that the Marines have not devoted sufficient thought to amphibious operations themselves. Understandably, the Marine Corps' visualization of an amphibious operation bears strong resemblance to those upon which it built its reputation and expertise during the Pacific War. It sees the problem essentially as one of coming ashore against opposition. Unless the operation is designated beforehand as a feint or demonstration, every effort is to be made to hold the beach once it is taken. It is a point of pride with Marines that they were never driven off a beach during World War II.

Unfortunately, this is an overly narrow definition of amphibious operations. It was appropriate for World War II, where the objectives were Pacific islands. The small size of the islands gave the enemy the advantage of interior lines; he could generally have shifted the focus of his defense at least as rapidly as the Marines could have withdrawn from one beach, reorganize for a second assault, and come ashore again somewhere else.

However, when considering large land masses such as the shores of the Persian Gulf or Indian Ocean, the situation may be quite different. Especially where overland communications are restricted by bad roads and difficult terrain, the seaborne force may in effect enjoy "interior lines." It may have greater relative mobility at sea than the opposing force has moving overland. The key to an ability to operate in this manner is an ability to keep the logistics base of the land force at sea. Although the Marine battalion with the Sixth Fleet already does this, using the Sea-based Mobile Logistics System, most Marine amphibious planning calls for moving the logistics ashore. Once this is done, the opponent has the necessary "hold" on the landing force. It will seldom be possible to evacuate a cumbersome logistical "tail" very rapidly, yet its abandonment and loss would render the fighting force useless. Thus, the landing force must stay and fight, even if it would gain operational advantages by returning to sea and attacking again somewhere else.

Sea basing of the logistics of the ground force is necessary for another reason as well. As noted, the ultimate loser in a Third World conflict will be the party that succeeds in arousing the local nationalism most strongly against itself. For forces from outside the local areas, this will tend to be the party which has the highest profile; for most locals, to see the outsider is to dislike him.

If our land force requires a Vietnam-like logistical tail, with its "little America" base camps, its prostitution parlors and currency inflation, and its constant friction with the local culture, then we are likely to end up the losers even if we win some battles along the way. The forces ashore must maintain a low profile. They must make do with the absolute minimum of personnel, and those personnel must have the least possible contact with the local inhabitants. Again, this requires keeping the logistics at sea.

Developing a sea-based logistical infrastructure will not be easy. It will require a major change on the part of the Navy: Amphibious ships and their escorts will no longer be able to drop the Marines on the beach and leave; they will need to remain close enough to the land operation to provide logistical support. However, a number of important tools seem readily available. They include:

(1) Helicopters. Not only can helicopters move people and basic supplies, they can also ferry many kinds of equipment. One Marine Corps requirement for the lightweight armored vehicles is that they be helicopter transportable. Helicopters can provide an "air bridge" between the forces ashore and their seaborne logistical and maintenance base.

(2) The ability to use merchant ships as air-capable ships. In project ARAPAHO, the Navy is developing an ability to convert merchant marine containerships to mini-aircraft carriers. The support facilities for the aircraft are containerized, and a Fairey girder bridge is laid atop the stacked containers to serve as a landing pad for helicopters and VSTOL aircraft, notably the Advanced Harrier (AV-8B), which the Corps is slated to acquire. The same concept could permit merchant ships to serve as depots and even repair facilities, with helicopters serving as the "trucks."

(3) The adoption of Soviet-model maintenance philosophies, in which the equipment is designed to run virtually without maintenance for a certain period or number of miles, after which it is automatically sent to depot. This approach would help orderly scheduling of sea-to-shore and shore-to-sea equipment moves. It would fit in well with maritime prepositioning, which is an equivalent of Soviet depot storage, and with maneuver warfare, where individual campaigns tend to be of short duration.

(4) The Field Logistics System. This new program will "containerize" virtually all Marine Corps logistics. The containers not only facilitate rapid movement between ship and shore, but should permit the facilities themselves to be made operational at sea, on containerships or small carriers such as the proposed VSTOL Support Ship/Landing Ship, Helicopter (LH-X/VSS).

(5) The Sea-based Mobile Logistics System. This containerized logistics system is currently utilized by Marines with the Sixth Fleet. An expanded version could assist in supporting sizable forces ashore.

(6) The return to service of one or more hospital ships.

(7) Finally, and perhaps most importantly, the logistical implications of maneuver warfare. As has been noted, the current enormous logistical tail of American forces traces in large part to their firepower/attrition doctrine. In this doctrine, logistics are sized on the assumption that, at any given time, most or all combat units are on line, engaged heavily with the enemy. Accordingly, organic sustaining capability is very high. In contrast, in maneuver warfare, the assumption is that, at any given time, most units are in reserve. Organic support is much less, and the ratio of combat to logistics elements is much higher. This, and not some "peasant hardiness" of the Russian soldier, is why the Soviet army has such a high ratio of combat to support compared with the American army. The RDF, with a maneuver doctrine, can plan on a much smaller "tail" than is traditional with American forces, which of course both assists directly in maintaining a low profile and helps in keeping the logistics sea-based.

Increasing Forcible-Entry Capabilities

Essential to any credible U.S. intervention force in the Persian Gulf is a robust U.S. forcible-entry capability. As noted in the preceding chapter, the present level of U.S. amphibious shipping is less than one-half that of the planning requirement specified by the Joint Chiefs of Staff; and naval gunfire support capabilities have been permitted to dwindle to patently unacceptable levels. The author believes that serious consideration should be given to expanding the level of amphibious shipping from the present 1.15-MAF lift capability to a minimum 2.33-MAF lift capability—the JCS planning requirement. A 2.33-MAF capability would permit the uninterrupted deployment in the Indian Ocean (or other Third World crisis areas) of at least one full amphibious assault brigade (compared with the present occasional visits of a battalion-sized landing force) as well as sufficient redundancy for larger assault operations.

As for naval gunfire support, the author would note that the U.S. Navy still retains in reserve some four *Iowa*-class battleships (mounting nine 16-inch guns apiece) and two *Salem*-class heavy cruisers (each with nine automatic 8-inch guns). The reactivation and refurbishment of one or more of these vessels would certainly enhance Marine Corps forcible-entry capabilities against lightly or even moderately defended beaches, if not against heavily defended shores.[117] The presence in the Indian

---

[117]During the Pacific campaign of World War II, large-caliber naval gunfire proved relatively ineffective against prepared, entrenched Japanese shore defense systems, characterized by extensive networks of well-camouflaged concrete bunkers and underground troop billets and ammunition storage areas. Such defenses, however, require enormous time and engineering resources to construct; they are not likely to be encountered along the extensive littorals of the Arabian peninsula.

Ocean of such vessels, with their awesome and easily visible capacity for destruction, also would contribute to deterrence.

The realization of many of the measures proposed above would entail substantial expenditures. Doubling the size of the U.S. amphibious fleet; recalling battleships or heavy cruisers to active service; procuring lightweight armor, additional logistics ships, helicopters and VSTOL aircraft; converting merchant vessels into mini-aircraft carriers—all are multi-billion dollar propositions. Moreover, the U.S. Navy's inability to recruit and retain sufficient numbers of qualified personnel to man the present 430-ship fleet suggests that the expansion in U.S. sea power necessary to provide a credible Rapid Deployment Force (current plans call for a 550-ship fleet by the mid-1980s and do not encompass increases in amphibious lift or the recall of ships from reserve) cannot be achieved within the framework of the All-Volunteer Force.

If, however, the United States is serious about mounting a convincing military defense of threatened Western interests in the Persian Gulf, it cannot avoid hard budgetary and social choices. The decision to commit the United States to a defense of those interests has already been made; what is lacking is the ability to do so.

Postscript

The foregoing critical analysis of the Rapid Deployment Joint Task Force was published by the Institute in February 1981, less than one month after the Reagan Administration was inaugurated. Unfortunately, the Administration to date has proved no more successful than its predecessor in resolving the serious problems confronting the RDJTF as an instrument of U.S. military intervention in the peculiar political and operational environments of Southwest Asia.

The one prominent exception has been the Administration's success in smoothing out the RDJTF's tangled command relationships. Shortly after taking office, Secretary of Defense Caspar W. Weinberger severed the highly unpleasant command relationship between the RDJTF and the U.S. Readiness Command. On January 1, 1983, the RDJTF (renamed the U.S. Central Command for reasons that remain a mystery) was established as a separate command reporting directly to the Secretary of Defense through the Joint Chiefs of Staff. The new command's responsibilities are restricted exclusively to Southwest Asia, although the Indian Ocean remains under the "jurisdiction" of the U.S. Pacific Command.

Against this notable success must be weighed some larger failures. In terms of the RDJTF's basic structure and underlying concept of operations, the Reagan Administration has more or less accepted what it inherited from the Carter Administration: a distant, excessively large, logistically ponderous intervention force dependent on uncontested access ashore, and dedicated in the first instance to defeating overt, massive Soviet aggression in Iran. Forces assigned to the RDJTF remain dual-committed to Europe and the Far East, imposing grave strategic risks for the United States in the event of a protracted, worldwide war with the Soviet Union of the kind delineated by the Reagan Administration as the basis for U.S. conventional force planning.

Although in 1982 the Administration did succeed in obtaining Congressional authorization for the first of a planned procurement of 50 new C-5B strategic air transports, and has managed (with some slight changes) to sustain budgetary support for inherited strategic sealift programs and to increase the size of the Near-Term Prepositioned Ship force, the large gap between RDJTF strategic mobility requirements and resources will persist indefinitely.

Nor has the Administration found a way to gain politically secure military access ashore in Southwest Asia in peacetime, which is vital to the RDJTF as it is now configured. Potential host governments in the region remain unwilling to permit the establishment on their territory of anything smacking of a permanent U.S. combat presence. Understandings and agreements for contingent rights of access with Egypt, Kenya, Somalia and Oman remain in effect, and since early 1981 RDJTF units have participated in exercises in Egypt and Oman, gaining valuable operational insights. Yet, an Administration campaign to establish ashore even a small advanced operational headquarters for the RDJTF has proved fruitless. The alternative of establishing such a headquarters afloat is opposed by the RDJTF's new commander, Army Lieutenant General Robert C. Kingston.

Indeed, although (as argued by the author in 1981) the lack of politically secure military access ashore virtually dictates an initial heavy reliance on on-the-spot, sea-based intervention forces with robust forcible-entry capabilities, the Reagan Administration, like its predecessor, plans no significant increases in amphibious shipping or sea-based logistical support capabilities. Naval gunfire support capabilities are to be increased through the recall to active service of as many as four *Iowa*-class battleships (one has already been recommissioned); Navy ship rotation policies, however, make it unlikely that more than one battleship would be available in a sudden crisis. Of perhaps even greater significance was the Administration's decision in 1982 to reduce the standing U.S. naval presence in the Indian Ocean from two carrier battlegroups to one.

Jeffrey Record
March 30, 1983

INSTITUTE FOR FOREIGN POLICY ANALYSIS, INC.
List of Publications

Special Reports

THE CRUISE MISSILE: BARGAINING CHIP OR DEFENSE BARGAIN? By Robert L. Pfaltzgraff, Jr., and Jacquelyn K. Davis. January 1977. x, 53pp. $3.00.

EUROCOMMUNISM AND THE ATLANTIC ALLIANCE. By James E. Dougherty and Diane K. Pfaltzgraff. January 1977. xiv, 66pp. $3.00.

THE NEUTRON BOMB: POLITICAL, TECHNICAL AND MILITARY ISSUES. By S. T. Cohen. November 1978. xii, 95pp. $6.50.

SALT II AND U.S.-SOVIET STRATEGIC FORCES. By Jacquelyn K. Davis, Patrick J. Friel and Robert L. Pfaltzgraff, Jr. June 1979. xii, 51pp. $5.00.

THE EMERGING STRATEGIC ENVIRONMENT: IMPLICATIONS FOR BALLISTIC MISSILE DEFENSE. By Leon Gouré, William G. Hyland and Colin S. Gray. December 1979. xi, 75pp. $6.50.

THE SOVIET UNION AND BALLISTIC MISSILE DEFENSE. By Jacquelyn K. Davis, Uri Ra'anan, Robert L. Pfaltzgraff, Jr., Michael J. Deane and John M. Collins. March 1980. xi, 71pp. $6.50. (Out of print.)

ENERGY ISSUES AND ALLIANCE RELATIONSHIPS: THE UNITED STATES, WESTERN EUROPE AND JAPAN. By Robert L. Pfaltzgraff, Jr. April 1980. xii, 71pp. $6.50.

U.S. STRATEGIC-NUCLEAR POLICY AND BALLISTIC MISSILE DEFENSE: THE 1980S AND BEYOND. By William Schneider, Jr., Donald G. Brennan, William A. Davis, Jr., and Hans Rühle. April 1980. xii, 61pp. $6.50.

THE UNNOTICED CHALLENGE: SOVIET MARITIME STRATEGY AND THE GLOBAL CHOKE POINTS. By Robert J. Hanks. August 1980. xi, 66pp. $6.50.

FORCE REDUCTIONS IN EUROPE: STARTING OVER. By Jeffrey Record. October 1980. xi, 92pp. $6.50.

SALT II AND AMERICAN SECURITY. By Gordon J. Humphrey, William R. Van Cleave, Jeffrey Record, William H. Kincade, and Richard Perle. October 1980. xvi, 65pp.

THE FUTURE OF U.S. LAND-BASED STRATEGIC FORCES. By Jake Garn, J. I. Coffey, Lord Chalfont, and Ellery B. Block. December 1980. xvi, 80pp.

THE CAPE ROUTE: IMPERILED WESTERN LIFELINE. By Robert J. Hanks. February 1981. xi, 80pp. $6.50 (Hardcover, $10.00).

THE RAPID DEPLOYMENT FORCE AND U.S. MILITARY INTERVENTION IN THE PERSIAN GULF. By Jeffrey Record. February 1981. viii, 82pp. $7.50 (Hardcover, $12.00).

POWER PROJECTION AND THE LONG-RANGE COMBAT AIRCRAFT: MISSIONS, CAPABILITIES, AND ALTERNATIVE DESIGNS. By Jacquelyn K. Davis and Robert L. Pfaltzgraff, Jr. June 1981. ix, 37pp. $6.50.

THE PACIFIC FAR EAST: ENDANGERED AMERICAN STRATEGIC POSITION. By Robert J. Hanks. October 1981. ix, 75pp. $7.50.

NATO'S THEATER NUCLEAR FORCE MODERNIZATION PROGRAM: THE REAL ISSUES. By Jeffrey Record. November 1981. vii, 102pp. $7.50.

THE CHEMISTRY OF DEFEAT: ASYMMETRIES IN U.S. AND SOVIET CHEMICAL WARFARE POSTURES. By Amoretta M. Hoeber. December 1981. xiii, 91pp. $6.50.

THE HORN OF AFRICA: A MAP OF POLITICAL-STRATEGIC CONFLICT. By James E. Dougherty. April 1982. xv, 74pp. $7.50.